# simple stylish
# CROCHET

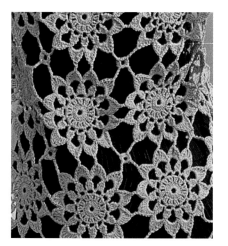

# simple stylish
# CROCHET

## A fabulous collection of
## 24 fashionable and fun designs

## Melody Griffiths

NEW
HOLLAND

First published in 2006 by
New Holland Publishers (UK) Ltd
London · Cape Town · Sydney · Auckland

Garfield House, 86–88 Edgware Road
London W2 2EA
United Kingdom
www.newhollandpublishers.com

80 McKenzie Street
Cape Town 8001
South Africa

Level 1, Unit 4, 14 Aquatic Drive
Frenchs Forest, NSW 2086
Australia

218 Lake Road
Northcote, Auckland
New Zealand

ISBN 1 84537 079 1

Senior Editor: Clare Sayer
Production: Hazel Kirkman
Design: Isobel Gillan
Photographer: Sian Irvine
Editorial Direction: Rosemary Wilkinson

10 9 8 7 6 5 4 3 2 1

Reproduction by Pica Digital PTE Ltd, Singapore
Printed and bound in Malaysia by Times Offset

# CONTENTS

# INTRODUCTION

Couture crochet, easy crochet, fun accessories or funky garments – everywhere you look fashion takes a fancy to this exciting craft. You too can create unusual, individual clothes with this collection of 24 up-to-the-minute styles, specially designed to be easy-to-make and wonderful to wear.

Crochet is one of the most rewarding and creative of the traditional crafts. The stitches are easy to learn and the materials are easy to find. All you need is a crochet hook and some yarn but the effects can vary enormously, from a lightweight lacy look to a densely textured surface.

All crochet stitches are based on the simple action of making loops with the hook, so once you've got the hang of this you'll find it surprisingly easy to master the different stitches and to create exciting, unusual things to wear.

Crochet is a two-handed craft with the left hand tensioning the yarn and holding the work while the right hand uses the hook. Because the left hand does a lot of work, most left-handed people find that they are comfortable working this way but if preferred, left-handers could reverse the actions, reading left for right and right for left, using a mirror if necessary to check the illustrations.

# BASIC INFORMATION

## Equipment

Crochet is an incredibly versatile craft – you can achieve the most wonderful effects with the simplest of materials. All you really need is a crochet hook but you may find some other sewing essentials useful.

### CROCHET HOOKS

The one essential piece of equipment you need to crochet is a crochet hook. The smallest size hooks are generally made of steel and come in sizes 0.60 mm to 2.50 mm. They are mostly used for delicate lace work using very fine yarns. Medium size hooks between 2.00 mm and 6.00 mm are usually made of coated aluminium or, in sizes 2.00 mm to 5.00 mm, bamboo. Large hooks in sizes 6.00 mm to 15.00 mm are made of plastic and may be hollow to reduce the weight. Old hooks may be bone, ivory or Bakelite. Even if only one hook size is given in the instructions to make a garment, it's a good idea to buy the size above and the size below as well because you may need to change hook size to obtain the correct tension (see page 10).

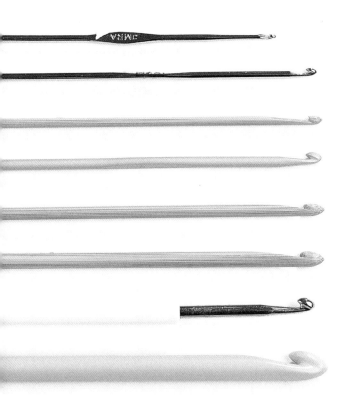

### CROCHET HOOK CONVERSION CHART
**Approximate sizes**

| Metric | Old UK | USA |
|---|---|---|
| 1.75 mm | 15 or 2½ or 3 | 5 or 6 |
| 2.00 mm | 14 or 1½ or 1 | 1 or B |
| 2.50 mm | 12 or 0 or 2/0 | 2 or C |
| 3.00 mm | 10 or 11 or 3/0 | 3 or D |
| 3.50 mm | 9 | 4 or E |
| 4.00 mm | 8 | 5 or F |
| 4.50 mm | 7 | 6 or G |
| 5.00 mm | 6 | 8 or H |
| 5.50 mm | 5 | 9 or I |
| 6.00 mm | 4 | 10 or J |
| 6.50 mm | 3 | |
| 7.00 mm | 2 | 10½ or K |
| 7.50 mm | 1 | 11 |
| 8.00 mm | 0 | 12 |
| 9.00 mm | 000 | 15 |

## OTHER EQUIPMENT

As well as range of hooks, other items you'll need to make garments are a tape measure, markers, pins, a blunt-pointed sewing needle or a tapestry needle and scissors.

## Yarns

The projects in this book use a wide range of yarns. Classic crochet uses smooth yarn and this is probably the best choice for a beginner as it is easier to see the stitches but interesting effects can be obtained with the simplest of stitches and unusual, textured fashion yarns. Each project has been designed specifically for the yarn given in the instructions. This is not to say that the designs cannot be made using an alternative but yarns vary so much that the you may not get the correct tension, the amount of yarn you need to buy could be different and the fabric you make may not behave in the same way as the original. Your choice could be a triumph but it could be a disaster, so if you do use a different yarn, be prepared for a different result. The fibre content and approximate yardages of the yarns used in this book are listed below.

**Coats Anchor Arista:** 80% viscose, 20 polyester. 100 m/110 yd per 25 g (1 oz) ball.

**Debbie Bliss Cashmerino Aran:** 55% merino, 33% microfibre, 12% cashmere. 90 m/98 yd per 50 g (1¾ oz) ball.

**Debbie Bliss Cathay:** 50% cotton, 35% microfibre, 15% silk. 100 m/110 yd per 50 g (1¾ oz) ball.

**Debbie Bliss Cotton Angora:** 80% cotton, 20% angora. 90 m/98 yd per 50 g (1¾ oz) ball.

**Debbie Bliss Cotton Cashmere:** 85% cotton, 15% cashmere. 95 m/104 yd per 50 g (1¾ oz) ball.

**Debbie Bliss Maya:** 100% wool slub. 126 m/137 yd per 100 g (3½ oz) ball.

**Debbie Bliss Merino DK:** 100% wool. 100 m/110 yd per 50 g (1¾ oz) ball.

**Elle True Blue DK:** 100% cotton. 108 m/118 yd per 50 g (1¾ oz) ball.

**Noro Kureyon:** 100% wool. 100 m/110 yd per 50 g (1¾ oz) ball.

**Patons Cotton 4 Ply:** 100% cotton. 330 m/361 yd per 100 g (3½ oz) ball.

**Patons Diploma Gold DK:** 55% wool, 25% acrylic, 20% nylon. 120 m/131 yd per 50 g (1¾ oz) ball.

**Rowan Big Wool:** 100% merino wool. 80 m/87 yd per 100 g (3½ oz) ball.

**Rowan Kidsilk Haze:** 70% super kid mohair, 30% silk. 210 m/229 yd per 25 g (1 oz) ball.

**Rowan Lurex Shimmer:** 80% viscose, 20% polyester. 95 m/103 yd per 25 g (1 oz) ball.

**Sirdar Bigga:** 50% wool, 50% acrylic. 40 m/44 yd per 100 g (3½ oz) ball.

**Sirdar Country Style DK:** 45% acrylic, 40% nylon, 15% wool. 318 m/347 yd per 100 g (3½ oz ball).

**Sirdar Fresco:** 100% nylon. 128 m/140 yd per 50 g (1¾ oz) ball.

**Sirdar Funky Fur:** 100% polyester. 90 m/98 yd per 50 g (1¾ oz) ball.

**Sirdar Wow!:** 100% polyester. 58 m/63 yd per 100 g (3½ oz) ball.

**Sirdar Duet:** 56% cotton, 44% nylon. 30 m/142 yd per 50 g (1¾ oz) ball.

**Sirdar Yo-Yo:** 74% acrylic, 14% wool, 12% polyester. 880 m/962 yd per 400 g (14 oz) ball.

# Getting Started

## FOLLOWING THE INSTRUCTIONS

Crochet instructions are really very easy to follow, once you familiarize yourself with the way they are set out. Before you start to crochet your garment, read through the instructions and make sure you understand what to expect. Make sure that you have the right yarn and a selection of crochet hooks. Check that you know what measurements you are working to – the 'to fit' sizes are provided as a guide but it is always a good idea to check that you will be happy with the finished actual measurements as the amount of movement room varies according to the design. If in doubt about which size to make, compare the actual measurements with a garment you already have and like. Where instructions for different sizes are given, figures are given for the smallest size first and the larger sizes, separated by colons, follow in brackets.

Abbreviations are used for many of the repetitive words that occur in crochet instructions. See right for a list of the most frequently used abbreviations; any additional abbreviations will be given with each individual pattern.

Square brackets are used where a set of instructions needs to be worked a number of times. For example: [3 tr in next ch sp] twice. This means that the instructions within the brackets are worked twice. Brackets can also be used to clarify working a group of stitches.

Stitch counts are also given at intervals throughout the pattern, often at the end of a row or round. These are set in square brackets.

Asterisks are used to indicate repetition of a sequence of instructions.

## READING STITCH DIAGRAMS

Where appropriate, stitch diagrams are also given. The stitch diagrams conform to the international symbols, with a few variations to explain individual stitches. The diagrams should be read in rows or in rounds exactly as the crochet is worked. Each stitch is represented by a symbol placed to create a picture of the stitch pattern, although occasionally symbols will have been stretched

| ABBREVIATIONS | | | |
|---|---|---|---|
| beg | beginning | rep | repeat |
| ch | chain | RS | right side |
| cont | continue | sp(s) | space(s) |
| dc | double crochet | ss | slip stitch |
| dec | decreas(e)(ing) | st(s) | stitch(es) |
| dtr | double treble | tog | together |
| foll | following | tr | treble |
| htr | half treble | trtr | triple treble |
| inc | increas(e)(ing) | WS | wrong side |
| patt | pattern | yrh | yarn around hook |

or compressed for the sake of clarity. The purpose of the stitch diagrams is to provide a quick visual reference as it is often a lot easier to recognise that five bars across a T mean wrap the yarn around the hook five times at the start of the stitch rather than trying to remember what 'quintr' means. However, the written instructions are complete as they stand and all the projects can be completed without the stitch diagrams. Each stitch diagram will have a key: the standard symbols for the basic stitches are listed below:

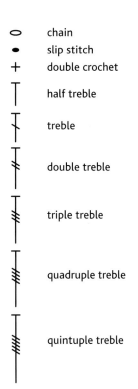

chain
slip stitch
double crochet
half treble
treble
double treble
triple treble
quadruple treble
quintuple treble

## CHECKING YOUR TENSION

Making sure that you have the correct tension is extremely important as the finished item will look very different from the original if you don't get this right. Although each pattern states which hook size you should use, tensions can vary so it is intended as guide only. Always change the hook size and try again if you do not achieve the tension given. Tensions in crochet seem to vary a great deal, probably because the stitch size is governed equally by the tension of the yarn in your fingers and the size of the hook. You are probably desperate to get on with making you garment but if you do not match the tension, your garment will end up either too tight or too loose.

The stitches at the edge can distort, so the best way to check your tension is to work a few more stitches and rows than given for a 10-cm (4-in) square, then to count and mark the number of stitches and rows needed. Measure between markers or long pins. If you get more than 10 cm (4 in), your crochet is too loose. Try again using a smaller hook. If you get less than 10 cm (4 in), your work is too tight. Try again using a larger hook.

## Basic techniques

### MAKING A SLIP KNOT

Most projects start with a slip knot.

Make a loop in the yarn, quite near the end. Insert the hook, catch the yarn and pull a loop through. Pull gently on both ends to tighten the knot and to close the loop on the hook.

### HOLDING THE HOOK

Most hooks have a flattened area a little way down from the hooked end which helps you to find the best place for your fingers and makes the hook more comfortable to hold. You can hold the hook like a pencil with the rounded end above your hand or like a knife with the end under your hand. Most people find the pencil grip more flexible but do experiment to find which suits you. However you hold the hook, your grip should be light so you can easily extend the hook in a forwards and back motion.

## HOLDING THE YARN AND THE WORK

Hold the tail end of yarn from the slip knot between first finger and thumb of your left hand. As the work grows, move the work to keep the thumb and first finger grip near the place that a new stitch will be made. The yarn lies over the middle and third fingers and is then wrapped around the little finger to tension it. For extra control, to tighten a loose tension or if working with fine or slippery yarns, wrap the yarn around the middle finger as well. Extending the middle finger lifts the yarn and makes it easy to catch the yarn with the hook.

## CHAIN STITCH (ch)

Chain stitch may be used as a foundation for other stitches, to make spaces or arches between stitches or to reach the height of the other stitches when working in rounds or turning and working in rows.

With a slip knot on the hook, take the hook in front of the yarn, dip the tip to take the yarn over the hook from back to front and draw a new loop through the loop on the hook. Repeat for each chain stitch.

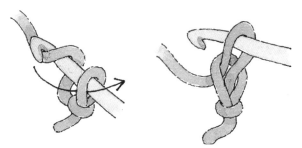

Here's a guide to the number of turning chain usually needed to give the correct height for some of the most often used stitches.

| | |
|---|---|
| Double crochet | 1 chain |
| Half treble | 2 chains |
| Treble | 3 chains |
| Double treble | 4 chains |

## SLIP STITCH (ss)

Slip stitch is the shortest stitch. It's used mostly for joining stitches or to carry the yarn along an edge when shaping or to a new place in the stitch pattern to avoid having to break off and rejoin the yarn.

Insert hook into stitch, dip the tip of the hook to wrap the yarn over from back to front and draw a new loop through both the stitch and the loop on the hook, so ending with one loop on the hook. The steps show joining a length of chain in a ring but the action is the same when working into any stitch.

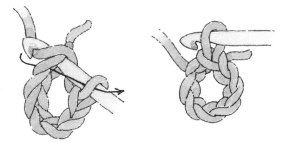

## DOUBLE CROCHET (dc)

Double crochet is like a slip stitch with an extra step. Depending on the yarn and hook size used, it can make a firm fabric when used alone. Double crochet can also be used with other stitches to link chains or to create stitch patterns. In this book, a single chain is worked at the start of each double crochet row but this chain is not worked into on the following row and it is not counted as a stitch. Some interesting variations on double crochet are Solomon's knot, crab stitch and loop stitch (see page 13).

Insert hook into chain or stitch indicated in the instructions, dip the tip of the hook to wrap the yarn around from back to front and draw the yarn through the stitch to make two loops on hook. Dip the tip of the hook to wrap the yarn around from back to front and draw the yarn through the two loops on the hook, so ending with one loop on the hook.

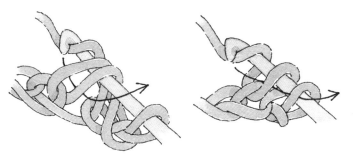

## Tips

- *When working into the base chain, take the hook under two strands of each chain loop unless instructed otherwise.*
- *Wherever possible, join in new yarn at the start of a row, using the same method as changing colours.*
- *Try to work your base chain stitches quite loosely. If they are tight it will be difficult to work into them and the edge will pull in. To work an even, loose chain, try using a hook that is one or two sizes larger.*

### TREBLE CROCHET (tr)

Treble is like double crochet but with an extra step. It is probably the most frequently used stitch, when used alone it makes a light, flexible fabric and can be combined with other stitches in groups, fans, clusters, mesh and openwork effects. Treble rows usually start with three chain to bring the yarn up to the height of the row, this counts as a stitch and the first stitch of the previous row is missed to compensate. However, this can leave a gap between the first and second stitches so depending on the design, often the first chain is replaced with a double crochet worked directly into the first stitch.

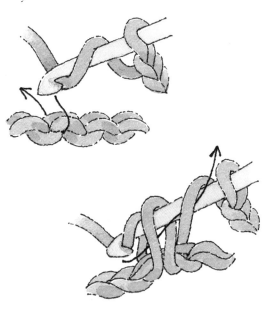

With the hook in front of the yarn, dip the tip of the hook to wrap the yarn around from back to front. Insert hook into chain or stitch indicated in the instructions, dip the tip of the hook to wrap the yarn around from back to front and draw the yarn through the stitch to make three loops on the hook. Dip the tip of the hook to wrap the yarn around from back to front and draw the yarn through the first two loops on the hook, wrap the yarn around the hook again and draw it through the two loops, so ending with one loop on the hook.

A half treble (htr) is worked in the same way as a treble up to the second step illustrated left, then the yarn is pulled through the new loop, the wrapped yarn and the original loop all in one movement to make a stitch that's between double crochet and treble in height.

### WORKING LONGER STITCHES

Double treble (dtr), triple treble (trtr), quadruple treble (quadtr) and quintuple treble (quintr) are all worked in the same way as a treble but the stitches are made longer with one more wrapping of the yarn around the hook before you start, so giving one more step when drawing through the loops at the end. The symbols show an extra bar for each time you wrap the yarn around the hook. Different height stitches are often combined to create a petal shape.

Here's a guide for the number of times to wrap the yarn around the hook when making longer stitches.

| | |
|---|---|
| Double treble | twice |
| Triple treble | three times |
| Quadruple treble | four times |
| Quintuple treble | five times |

## Variations on standard stitches

### INSERTING THE HOOK

All the standard stitches are worked either under two strands of the starting chain or under both strands at the top of a stitch but there are variations in placing the hook which give different effects.

### Inserting the hook into one strand only

This can be either at the front or at the back of the stitch. This can be used practically, when working into both sides of a starting chain or decoratively, to open up a fabric.

### Inserting the hook between stitches

This opens up the fabric and may be quicker to work. It can be used if the fabric is too fine or firm to insert the hook in the usual way or it can be used to group more stitches than would fit comfortably in a normal stitch.

### Taking the hook around the stem of a stitch

This is called a raised stitch because it lies on the surface of the work. Prepare to make the stitch by wrapping the yarn around the hook as directed, take the hook in front of the work and insert it down before the stitch designated in the row below, then up after the stitch, complete the stitch in the usual way. Raised stitches can also be made on the back of the work.

### Inserting the hook in the side of a stitch

This is particularly useful when making a double or a treble chain. For a double chain, make a slip knot and two chains. Insert hook in first chain and work one double crochet stitch. For each following stitch, insert hook under the threads at the side of the previous stitch. For a treble chain, make a slip knot and three chains. Take the yarn around the hook, then insert hook in third chain and complete the treble in the usual way. For each following stitch, insert the hook under one or two of the strands at the bottom of the previous stitch. Double and treble chains make a more flexible edge than an ordinary starting chain, they are also easier to count.

## Variations on double crochet

### SOLOMON'S KNOT

This stitch is simply a chain stitch, elongated and secured with a double crochet stitch.

Pull up loop to length required, take the yarn around the hook and pull through making a loose

chain stitch. Insert hook in the back loop of the chain and work a double crochet stitch, this will lock the loose chain in place. Repeat and join knots as given in the instructions for the mohair wrap, page 104.

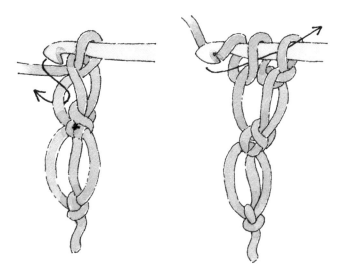

### CRAB STITCH

This is an excellent edging stitch. It is literally double crochet, worked backwards. It is best worked after a right side row of double crochet.

Do not turn the work at the end of the row. Insert the hook in the previous stitch, take the yarn around the hook and pull through to make two loops on the hook. Take the yarn around the hook again and pull through so one loop is left on the hook. Repeat along the edge. Crab stitch spreads the edge slightly so there's no need to increase to turn a corner. If the edge flutes, either skip the occasional stitch in the double crochet row or use a smaller hook.

### LOOP STITCH

This is really a double crochet stitch with the middle loop pulled out and locked with another stitch. It's always worked on wrong side rows, so the loop, which is made at the back of the work, is on the right side.

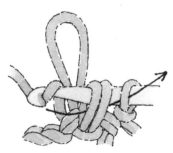

Insert hook. Extend middle finger to form a loop, take both threads of the loop around the hook and pull through to make three loops on the hook. Take the yarn around the hook, pull through the three loops on the hook and remove finger from loop. Keeping the middle finger of the left hand extended can be quite tiring, you may find it easier to transfer the extended loop to the middle finger of the right hand after pulling through to make three loops on the hook.

## Grouping stitches

Stitches of any length can be grouped or worked together to increase or decrease the number of stitches in a row or for a decorative effect. If complete stitches are worked into the same stitch a fan or increase is made, or they can be linked at the top to give a popcorn. If the stitches are worked in a row but joined at the top a cluster or decrease is made. Working stitches all in the same place and joining them at the top makes a bobble.

### FAN / INCREASE

Working two or more complete stitches into the same stitch in the row below can increase the number of stitches in a row or be used to make a fan stitch pattern.

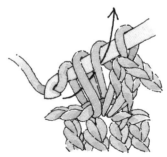

This example shows three treble stitches all worked into one treble in the row below. Simply work the trebles in the usual way but inserting the hook in the same stitch each time. Because the stitches are held together at the bottom but not at the top, working more then two or three stitches in the same place will give a fan shape.

## CLUSTER / DECREASE

Any combination of stitches can be joined together at the top by leaving the last loop of each stitch on the hook, then working all the loops together to complete the cluster. Clustering two or three stitches together can also be a way of decreasing.

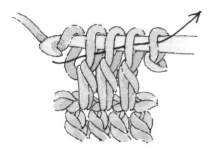

This example shows how three stitches can be clustered together. Leaving the last loop of each stitch on the hook, work a treble into each of the next three stitches, so making four loops on the hook. Take the yarn around the hook and pull through all four loops to join the stitches together at the top.

## BOBBLE

When a cluster is worked into one stitch, a bobble is made. If the stitches used for the bobble are longer than the background stitches, the bobble will stand away from the surface.

This example shows three trebles worked together. Wrap the yarn around the hook and insert hook in stitch. Take the yarn around the hook and pull through. Do not complete the treble, leave this last loop on the hook and continue working part trebles, each time leaving one more loop on the hook, in this case, until there are four loops on the hook including the original loop. Take the yarn around the hook and pull through all four loops.

BASIC INFORMATION

## POPCORN

This method makes a bobble that stands up from the surface without the need to make longer stitches. A popcorn can be placed in any stitch and be made up of any practical number or combination of stitches.

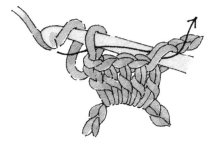

Here a five-treble popcorn is worked into a chain space. Inserting hook in same place each time, work five complete trebles. Lengthen the last loop slightly and slip the hook out. Insert the hook into the top of the first stitch, then into the last loop, take the yarn around the hook and pull through, tightening the stitch to make the popcorn stand up.

## MAKING GARMENTS

### WORKING IN ROWS

The fabric usually starts with a base chain, a double or treble chain or a picot row. Each row of the instructions will tell you where to place the hook and which stitch to work. Simply turn the work at the end of each row so the right and the wrong side face alternately. The instructions will tell you how many turning chain to work or how to cope with the edge stitches.

### WORKING IN ROUNDS

The fabric is worked from the centre outwards. The starting point can be a ring of chain or a loop ring. Chain gives a very firm start, loop rings can be neater and less obtrusive. A loop ring is made by working into yarn wound once around the left first finger, just like the first step in making a slip knot. The free end is worked over and pulled gently to close the ring when the first round of stitches has been completed.

When working in rounds, the right side always faces you. The instructions will tell you how to join at the end of each round and how many chain to work to match the height of the stitches in the next round.

## COLOUR CROCHET

Capital letters, A, B, C etc are used to designate the different colours. Because the last loop of a stitch forms the top of the next stitch, when changing colours, work the last stitch in the old colour until two loops remain on the hook, then use the new colour to complete the stitch. For some striped colour patterns, you can carry the yarn not in use up the side of the work, if this is not practical, cut the yarn and work over the ends. When working colour motifs, carry the yarn not in use along and slightly behind the top of the stitches in the row below and work over it until needed.

## MAKING UP

Some of the designs are worked in the round, so there is a minimum of making up to do. Garments worked in flat pieces can be sewn together or joined with crochet. Placing markers and pinning seams will help to match the rows and give a neater finish. If sewing, preferably, join the pieces with the right sides facing, matching the rows and taking in two threads of each stitch from each side rather than whole stitches to reduce the bulk. Alternatively, place the right sides together and oversew the seams.

Joining a seam with crochet gives a firm, neat chain edge. Insert the hook under an edge stitch from each side and work a slip stitch or a double crochet stitch. The instructions will tell you if the crochet seams are intended to be decorative and should be worked with the right side facing. If the ball band allows the yarn to be pressed, press the pieces, checking that they are the correct size. Press again after joining the shoulders and setting in the sleeves.

# CLASSIC

From classics with a twist to modern classics, these are clothes that are always in style. In this section you'll find projects to suit every look, from the generously sized denim duffle – which will be even better when worn and weathered – to the throwaway chic of a thirties-style boa, which takes just hours to make. In between there's a new look at old favourites, a patterned hat, a glorious poncho, the brightest chevron scarf, a shapely take on pioneer patchwork and a cropped zip jacket. Invest the time in creating these clever classics and you'll wear them time and time again.

*This casual coat is a classic that you'll wear and love forever. It's in a pure indigo dyed cotton yarn that will fade when washed so the texture of the stitches will be enhanced with time.*

# DENIM DUFFLE COAT

★ ☆ ☆ **VERY EASY**

🖐 *When working straight, the instructions give 1 dc and 2 ch at the beginning of a row instead of the usual 3 ch to help close the gap between the first and second stitches. The dc and 2 ch is counted as one stitch. When increasing, 3 turning chains are worked and a tr is worked into the first tr, so making one stitch.*

🖐 *Because it can be difficult to work the starting chain loosely even if you use a larger hook, the back and fronts are worked from the top downwards so the lower edge cannot pull in. The sleeves are worked from the cuff upwards so the softer finishing edge is at the top.*

## HELPFUL HINTS
- For a jacket without a hood you'll need approximately three less balls of yarn.
- When making a lot of chain, it can be difficult to count the stitches. If in doubt, add a few extra chains, it's easier to undo spare chain than to undo the first row to add more chain if you've miscounted.
- Elle True Blue is a 100% cotton indigo dyed yarn that is made to fade and shrinks by approximately 5% in length in the first wash. The measurements and tension given are for before washing.

## MEASUREMENTS
### To fit bust

| | | | | |
|---|---|---|---|---|
| 86–91 | 97–102 | 107–112 | 117–122 | cm |
| 34–36 | 38–40 | 42–44 | 46–48 | in |

### Actual bust

| | | | | |
|---|---|---|---|---|
| 115 | 125 | 135 | 145 | cm |
| 45¼ | 49¼ | 53 | 57 | in |

### Actual length

| | | | | |
|---|---|---|---|---|
| 70 | 70 | 83 | 83 | cm |
| 27½ | 27½ | 32½ | 32½ | in |

### Actual sleeve
51 cm
20 in

*In the instructions figures are given for the smallest size first; larger sizes follow in brackets. Where only one set of figures is given this applies to all sizes.*

## MATERIALS
- 19 (21:24:26) × 50 g balls of Elle True Blue DK in Denim 112
- 4.00 mm crochet hook
- 4 toggles

## TENSION
16 sts and 9 rows to 10 cm (4 in) measured over treble crochet before washing using 4.00 mm hook. Change hook size if necessary to obtain this tension.

## ABBREVIATIONS
**MB** – leaving last loop of each st on hook, work 5dtr all in same st, yrh and pull through all 6 loops on hook
**2trtog** – leaving last loop of each st on hook, work 1 tr in each of next 2 sts, yrh and pull though 3 loops on hook
*See also page 9.*

# DUFFLE COAT

### BOBBLE DIAMOND PANEL
Worked over 17 sts.
**Row 1:** (WS) MB, 1 tr in each of next 15 tr, MB.
**Row 2 and every RS row:** 1 tr in each of next 17 sts.
**Row 3:** MB, [1 tr in each of next 7 tr, MB] twice.

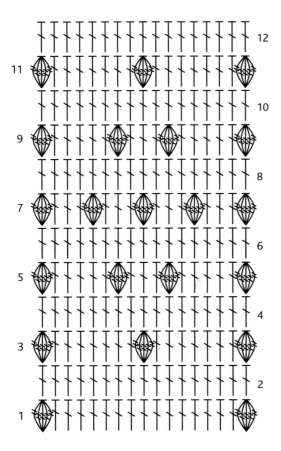

*Because the sleeve increases are on every 3rd row, they alternate between RS and WS rows but as the stitch pattern is the same on every row, the increases are made in the same way. Mark each increase row with a contrast loop of yarn to make it easier to keep track of them and also to make it easier to match the rows when sewing up.*

**Row 5:** MB, 1 tr in each of next 5 tr, MB, 1 tr in each of next 3 tr, MB, 1 tr in each of next 5 tr, MB.
**Row 7:** MB, [1 tr in each of next 3 tr, MB] 4 times.
**Row 9:** As Row 5.
**Row 11:** As Row 3.
**Row 12:** As Row 2.
Repeat these 12 rows for bobble diamond panel patt.

## RIGHT FRONT

Make 33 (37:39:43) ch.

### Shape neck

**Row 1:** (WS) 1 tr in 4th ch from hook, 1 tr in each ch to end. [31 (35:37:41) sts.]
**Row 2:** 1 dc in 1st tr, 2 ch, 1 tr in each tr to last st, 1 tr in 3rd ch **.
**Row 3:** 1 dc in 1st tr, 2 ch, 1 tr in each of next 2 (4:4:6) tr, work 17 sts of Row 1 of bobble diamond panel, 1 tr in each of next 10 (12:14:16) tr, 1 tr in 2nd ch.
**Row 4:** 1 dc in 1st tr, 2 ch, 1 tr in each st to last st, 2 tr in 2nd ch. [32 (36:38:42) sts.]
**Row 5:** 3 ch, 1 tr in 1st tr, 1 tr in each of next 3 (5:5:7) tr, work 17 sts of Row 3 of bobble diamond panel, 1 tr in each tr to last st, 1 tr in 2nd ch. [33 (37:39:43) sts.]
Cont in tr with bobble diamond panel as set, inc at neck edge in same way as Rows 4 and 5 on next 5 (5:7:7) rows, so ending with a RS row. [38 (42:46:50) sts.]

### Shape front neck

Do not turn after last row, make 12 ch, turn.
**Next row:** (WS) 1 tr in 4th ch from hook, 1 tr in each of next 8 ch, patt to end.
[48 (52:56:60) sts.]
Cont working bobble diamond panel patt with tr at each side for 52 (52:62:62) more rows, so ending with Row 1 of 6th (6th:7th:7th) bobble diamond panel patt. Fasten off.

## LEFT FRONT

Work as right front to **.

**Row 3:** (WS) 1 dc in 1st tr, 2 ch, 1 tr in each of next 10 (12:14:16) tr, work 17 sts of Row 1 of bobble diamond panel, 1 tr in each of next 2 (4:4:6) tr, 1 tr in 2nd ch.

**Row 4:** 3 ch, 1 tr in 1st tr, 1 tr in each st to last st, 1 tr in 2nd ch.
[32 (36:38:42) sts.]

**Row 5:** 1 dc in 1st tr, 2 ch, 1 tr in each of next 10 (12:14:16) tr, work 17 sts of Row 3 of bobble diamond panel, 1 tr in each of next 3 (5:5:7) tr, 2 tr in 3rd ch.
[33 (37:39:43) sts.]

Cont in tr with bobble diamond panel as set, inc at neck edge in same way as Rows 4 and 5 on next 5 (5:7:7) rows, so ending with a RS row. [38 (42:46:50) sts.]

### Shape front neck

Join a spare length of yarn at neck edge and make 10 ch.

**Next row:** (WS) 1 dc in 1st tr, 2 ch, patt to 10 ch, 1 tr in each of 10 ch.
[48 (52:56:60) sts.]

Cont working bobble diamond panel patt with tr at each side for 52 (52:62:62) more rows, so ending with Row 1 of 6th (6th:7th:7th) bobble diamond panel patt. Fasten off.

## BACK

Make 94 (102:110:118) ch.

**Row 1:** (WS) 1 tr in 4th ch from hook, 1 tr in each ch to end. [92 (100:108:116) sts.]

**Row 2:** 1 dc in 1st tr, 2 ch, 1 tr in each tr to last st, 1 tr in 3rd ch.

Row 2 forms tr patt. Working into 2nd ch for last st on foll rows, cont in tr for 61 (61:73:73) more rows. Fasten off.

## SLEEVES (MAKE 2)

Make 50 (54:58:62) ch.

**Row 1:** (RS) 1 tr in 4th ch from hook, 1 tr in each ch to end. [48 (52:56:60) sts.]

**Row 2:** 1 dc in 1st tr, 2 ch, 1 tr in each tr to last st, 1 tr in 3rd ch.

Cont in tr patt as given for back, work 1 row.

**Inc row:** 3 ch, 1 tr in 1st tr, 1 tr in each tr to last st, 2 tr in 2nd ch. [50 (54:58:62) sts.]

Cont in tr, inc in this way at each end of 13 foll 3rd rows. [76 (80:84:88) sts.]

Work 3 rows. Fasten off.

## HOOD

### Front

Make 131 (131:135:135) ch.

**Row 1:** (RS) 1 tr in 4th ch from hook, 1 tr in each ch to end. [129 (129:133:133) sts.]

Cont in tr patt as given for back, work 2 rows.

**Dec row:** 1 dc in 1st tr, 2 ch, 2trtog, 1 tr in each tr to last 3 sts, 2trtog, 1 tr in 2nd ch. [127 (127:131:131) sts.]

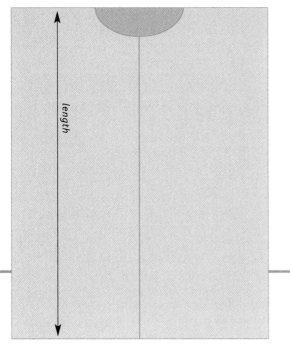

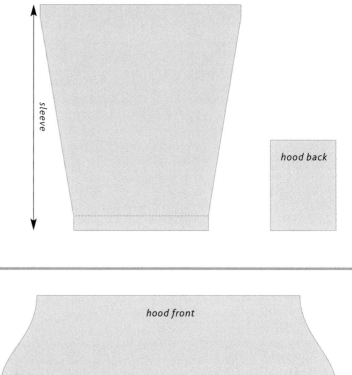

Cont in tr, dec in this way at each end of next 11 (11:13:13) rows. [105 sts.] Work 3 (3:4:5) rows. Fasten off.

### Back
Make 29 ch.

**Row 1:** (RS) 1 tr in 4th ch from hook, 1 tr in each ch to end. [27 sts.]

Cont in tr, work 19 more rows. Fasten off.

### TOGGLE LOOPS (MAKE 8)
Make 31 ch.

**Row 1:** 1 dc in 2nd ch from hook, 1 dc in each ch to end. [30 sts.] Fasten off.

### FRONT AND NECK EDGING
With WS together and back facing, matching sts, join right shoulder seam with dc. With WS together and back facing, join left shoulder seam in the same way. With RS facing, join yarn at right front lower edge.

**Row 1:** (RS) Work 106 (106:130:130) dc in row ends to right front neck, 30 (30:34:34) dc up right front neck, 30 (30:34:34) dc across back neck, 30 (30:34:34) dc down left front neck and 106 (106:130:130) dc in row ends down left front edge.

**Row 2:** 1 ch, 1 dc in each dc to left front neck, 2 dc in next dc, 1 dc in each dc to last dc around neck, 2 dc in next dc, 1 dc in each dc to end. Fasten off.

### TO MAKE UP
Join all seams with a row of dc to make a ridge on RS.

Place markers 24 (25:26.5:27.5) cm (9½ (9¾:10½:10¾) in) down from shoulders on back and fronts. Join sleeves between markers. Set back of hood into shorter edge of front of hood. Noting that seams of back of hood do not join to shoulder seams, join shaped edge of hood to neck edge. Join side and sleeve seams, reversing seam for turn back cuffs. Knot ends of toggle loops to make a neat bobble with a loop at folded end. Sew four loops on each front. Enclose a toggle in each loop on left front and stitch to secure.

*This hat is worked in the round from the top down. Changing colour to work the patterns is easier because the right side of the hat is always facing. The earflaps are worked in rows but there's a clever trick to making the double crochet fabric look the same as the rest of the hat.*

# INCA-STYLE EARFLAP HAT

★★☆ EASY

*Colour patterned crochet is easier to work in rounds because the yarn ends are always on the wrong side.*

## HELPFUL HINTS

- The hat is worked from the top down.
- Double crochet in rounds has a different appearance to double crochet worked in rows. To work a tension square, use the method of working rows that are all worked in the same direction as used for the earflaps or start the top of the hat and measure from the centre to the edge after 11 rounds. If this measures 6 cm (2½ in) and the circumference is 31.5 cm (12½ in), you can continue; if it is larger start again using a smaller hook, if it is smaller start again using a larger hook.
- Simply work over the yarn not in use to carry it along until needed.
- As a general rule, while increasing, change to B for last loop of last st in A but do not change A before completing last st of motif in B. When working straight, change colour for the last loop each time.
- Do not count the 1 ch at the start of the round as a stitch. Always work the first dc in the same place as the ss of the previous round.

## MEASUREMENTS

Actual measurement around head
58.5 cm
23 in

## MATERIALS

- 2 × 50 g balls of Debbie Bliss Cotton Cashmere in blue 12 (A)
- 1 × 50 g ball of Debbie Bliss Cotton Cashmere in pink 19 (B)
- 3.50 mm crochet hook

## TENSION

19 sts and 20 rows to 10 cm (4 in) measured over double crochet worked in rounds using 3.50 mm hook. Change hook size if necessary to obtain this tension.

## ABBREVIATIONS

**2dctog** – insert hook in first st, yrh and pull through, insert hook in second st, yrh and pull through, yrh and pull through 3 loops on hook *See also page 9.*

## EARFLAP HAT

### HAT

Wind A around finger to make a ring, insert hook and pull loop through.

**Round 1:** (RS) 3 ch, 11 tr in ring, pull end to close ring, ss in 3rd ch. [12 sts.]

**Round 2:** 1 ch, 1 dc in 3rd ch, 1 dc in each tr, ss in 1st dc. [12 sts.]

**Round 3:** Using A, work 1 ch, 2 dc in same place as ss, 2 dc in next dc, [2dcB in next dc, 2dcA in each of foll 2 dc] 3 times, 2dcB in next dc, ss in 1st dc. [24 sts.]

# TIP

For a tassel with a really nice round top, tie the strands in the centre in the usual way and fold in half, then thread a large wooden bead on to a few of the inner strands and push it to the top of the tassel. Arrange the other strands to cover the bead before wrapping the tie thread around below the bead and securing the end.

**Round 4:** 1chA, [1dcA in each of 3dc, 2dcB in next dc, 1dcB in foll dc, 2dcB in next dc] 4 times, ss in 1st dc. [32 sts.]

**Round 5:** 1chA, [1dcA in each of 2dc, 2dcB in next dc, 1dcB in each of foll 4dc, 2dcB in next dc] 4 times, ss in 1st dc. [40 sts.]

**Round 6:** 1chB, 1dcB in each of 5dc, [2dcA in next dc, 1dcB in each of 9dc] 3 times, 2dcA in next dc, 1dcB in each of 4dc, ss in 1st dc. [44 sts.]

**Round 7:** 1chB, 1dcB in each of 4dc, [1dcA in each of next 5dc, 1dcB in each of 6dc] 3 times, 1dcA in each of next 5dc, 1dcB in each of 2dc, ss in 1st dc.

**Round 8:** 1chB, 1dcB in each of 3dc, [1dcA in each of next 7dc, 1dcB in each of 4dc] 3 times, 1dcA in each of next 7dc, 1dcB in last dc, ss in 1st dc.

**Round 9:** 1chB, 1dcB in each of 2dc, [ * 2dcA in each of next 2dc, 1dcA in each of foll 5dc, 2dcA in each of next 2dc *, 1dcB in each of 2dc] 3 times, rep from * to *, ss in 1st dc. [60 sts.]

**Rounds 10 and 11:** Using A, work 2 rounds.

**Round 12:** Using B, 1 ch, [1 dc in each of next 5 dc, 2 dc in foll dc] 10 times, ss in 1st dc. [70 sts.]

**Round 13:** Using B, work 1 round.

**Rounds 14, 15, 16 and 17:** Work 4 rounds from Chart 1.

**Round 18:** Using A, 1 ch, 2 dc in 1st dc, [1 dc in each of next 4 dc, 2 dc in next dc] to last 4 dc, 1 dc in each dc, ss in 1st dc. [84 sts.]

**Round 19:** Using A, work 1 round.

**Round 20:** Using B, work 1 round.

**Round 21:** Using B, 1 ch, [1dcB, 1dcA] to end.

**Rounds 22 and 23:** Using A, work 2 rounds.

**Round 24:** Using A, 1 ch, [1 dc in each of next 6 dc, 2 dc in foll dc] 12 times, ss in 1st dc. [96 sts.]

**Round 25:** Using A, work 1 round.

**Round 26:** Using B, work 1 round.

**Round 27:** As round 21.

**Round 28:** Using A, work 1 round.

**Round 29:** Using A, 1 ch, [1 dc in each of next 5 dc, 2 dc in foll dc] 16 times, ss in 1st dc. [112 sts.]

**Round 30:** Using A, work 1 round.

**Rounds 31 to 40:** Work 10 rounds from Chart 2.

**Rounds 41 to 43:** Using A, work 3 rounds. Fasten off.

## RIGHT EARFLAP

Using A, join yarn in 14th dc from beg of round. 1 ch, 1 dc same dc as joined yarn, 1 dc in each of next 19 dc, fasten off by enlarging last loop, passing the ball of yarn through it and pulling yarn to close loop. [20 sts.] Lay the yarn along the edge of the work and join in first stitch.

**Next row:** (RS) 1 ch, working over yarn, work 1 dc in each dc to end, fasten off as before.

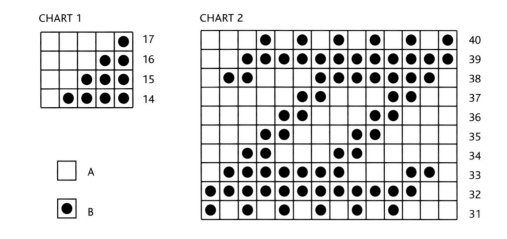

CHART 1

17 16 15 14

CHART 2

40 39 38 37 36 35 34 33 32 31

□ A

● B

Cont in dc fastening off at end of each row and working over yarn so RS is always facing, work 1 more row.

**Dec row:** (RS) 1 ch, miss 1st dc, 1 dc in each dc to last 2 dc, 2dctog. [18 sts.]

Cont in RS dc, dec in this way at each end of 3 foll 3rd rows, then at each end of next 3 rows. [6 sts.] Fasten off.

## LEFT EARFLAP

Miss centre 46 dc, join A in next dc and work as given for Right Earflap.

## EDGING

Join yarn A at beg of last round and work 1 round dc all around edge of hat.

**Next round:** Work as Round 21.

**Next round:** Using B work 1 round dc. Turn at end of round.

**Next round:** Using B and working 3 dc tog at each side of earflap to keep flaps flat, work 1 round dc. Fasten off.

## TO MAKE UP

Make a tassel using twenty-four 30-cm (12-in) long strands of B. Sew on top of hat.

# VARIATION

## ONE COLOUR HAT

If you want the hat in just one colour, simply follow the shaping as given but use just one colour, ignoring the colour changes and working the chart pattern rounds plain. You'll still need three balls of Debbie Bliss Cotton Cashmere in the colour of your choice.

*To work from charts, work in dc reading every line of chart from right to left.*

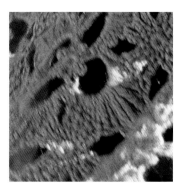

*There's just four rounds to each of the leaf motif blocks that are joined in a square to make this dramatic poncho.*

# LEAF MOTIF PONCHO

The poncho is made from 4-leaf motifs joined to form a square with the four motifs at the centre omitted to make the neck hole.

Instructions are given for making and joining all of the leaf motif blocks, then working all the filler motifs. If you prefer, you could work the filler motifs as you join the blocks.

You can work over the end of the 8-ch ring at the centre of the leaf motif block for a few stitches, then just snip it off but the end of each filler motif should be thoroughly darned in before trimming.

## HELPFUL HINTS

- Using different height stitches makes Round 3 of the motif grow really quickly. Here's a reminder of how many times to take the yarn around the hook before inserting the hook to work the stitches: dc = no times, htr = once but pull through all loops first time; tr = once; dtr = twice, trtr = 3 times; quadtr = 4 times, quintr = 5 times.
- Save making up time by darning in the ends as you join motifs.

## MEASUREMENTS

One size

**Actual width**

102 cm

40 in

**Actual length (from shoulder to point)**

72 cm

28¼ in

## MATERIALS

- 13 × 50 g balls of Patons Diploma Gold DK in Apple Green 06125
- 4.00 mm crochet hook

## TENSION

One leaf block measures 12.5 cm × 12.5 cm (5 × 5 in) when pressed, using 4.00 mm hook. Change hook size if necessary to obtain this tension.

## ABBREVIATIONS

**quadtr** – quadruple treble
**quintr** – quintuple treble
*See also page 9.*

## PONCHO

### LEAF MOTIF BLOCK

Make 8 ch, ss in 1st ch to form a ring.

**Round 1:** (RS) 7 ch, [2 dc in ring, 6 ch] 7 times, 2 dc in ring, ss in 1st ch, ss in each of next 2 ch.

**Round 2:** 1 ch, 2 dc in 1st 7-ch loop, [16 ch, miss next 6-ch loop, 3 dc in next 6-ch loop] 3 times, 16 ch, 1 dc in 1st 6-ch loop, ss in 1st dc.

**Round 3:** Work [2 dc, 2 htr, 2 tr, 2 dtr, 2 trtr, 2 quadtr, 1 quintr, 2 quadtr, 2 trtr, 2 dtr, 2 tr, 2 htr, 2 dc] in each 16-ch loop.

**Round 4:** * Ss in each of next 2 dc, [4 ch, ss in each of next 2 sts] 11 times, ss in last dc of leaf, rep from * 3 more times, ss in 1st ss. Fasten off.

### 1st line of blocks, second motif

Work as first motif to Round 4.

**Round 4:** * Ss in each of next 2 dc, [4 ch, ss in each of next 2 sts] 11 times, ss in last dc of leaf, rep from * once more, ** ss in each of next 2 dc, [4 ch, ss in each of next 2 sts] 5 times, with WS together join to 6th 4-ch loop at point of leaf of previous motif by working

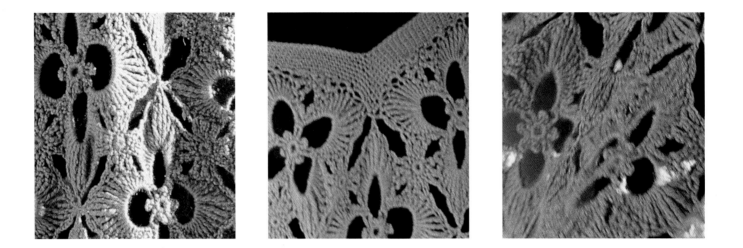

2 ch, dc in 4-ch loop, 2 ch, ss in each of next 2 sts, [4 ch, ss in each of next 2 sts] 5 times, ss in last dc of leaf, rep from ** once more, joining in 4-ch loop of next leaf of previous motif, ss in 1st ss. Fasten off.
Continue making and joining blocks in this way until 1st line of 8 blocks has been completed.

### 2nd and 3rd lines of blocks
Join 8 blocks in the same way but linking blocks to 4-ch loops of previous row as well as to each other.

### 4th and 5th lines of blocks
Join 3 blocks, omit centre two blocks, join 3 blocks.

### 6th, 7th and 8th lines of blocks
Join as 2nd line of blocks.

### BLOCK FILLER MOTIFS
Worked into centre three 4-ch sps of each of 4 leaves of adjacent blocks.
Loop yarn around first finger to make a ring.
**Round 1:** (RS) 1 ch, 12 dc in ring, pull end to close ring, ss in 1st dc.
**Round 2:** 2 ch, * 1 dc in 2nd 4-ch sp of 1st leaf, [2 ch, ss in next dc of 1st round, 2 ch, 1 dc in next 4-ch sp] twice, 2 ch, ss in next dc of 1st round, rep from * working into centre three 4-ch sps of each of next 3 leaves, ending

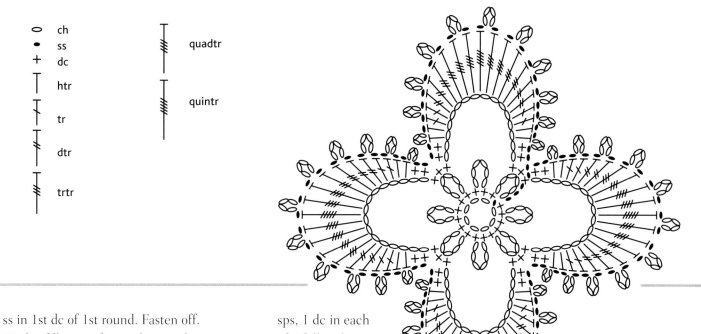

| Symbol | Stitch |
|---|---|
| ○ | ch |
| ● | ss |
| + | dc |
| T | htr |
| † | tr |
| ‡ | dtr |
| ‡ | trtr |
| ‡ | quadtr |
| ‡ | quintr |

ss in 1st dc of 1st round. Fasten off. Work a filler motif in each space between blocks.

## NECK FILLER MOTIFS

Work in same way as block filler motif but make only 9 dc in ring on 1st round and join into 2 leaves of motif only.

## NECKBAND

With RS facing, join yarn in a joined 4-ch sp at one corner of neck.

**Round 1:** (RS) 1 ch, [2 dc in 1st ch sp of block, 3 dc in each of next 3 ch sps, 1 dc in each of next 3 dc of filler motif, 3 dc in each of next 3 ch sps, 2 dc in foll ch sp] 8 times, ss in 1st dc. [200 sts.] Missing 1st dc, 2 dc at each corner and last dc on each round, work 7 rounds dc. [144 sts.] Fasten off.

## EDGING

With RS facing, join yarn in joined 4-ch sp of 2nd block along from one corner of outer edge of poncho.

**Round 1:** (RS) 1 ch, * [1 dc in joined 4-ch sp, 4 dc in each of next four 4-ch sps, 1 dc in each of 2 foll 4-ch sps, 4 dc in each of next four 4-ch sps, 1 dc in joined 4-ch sp] 6 times, 1 dc in joined 4-ch sp, 4 dc in each of next four 4-ch sps, 1 dc in each of 2 foll 4-ch sps, 4 dc in each of next four 4-ch sps, 7 dc in corner 4-ch sp, 4 dc in each of next four 4-ch

sps, 1 dc in each of 2 foll 4-ch sps, 4 dc in each of next four 4-ch sps, 1 dc in joined 4-ch sp, rep from * 3 more times, ss in 1st dc. Fasten off.

## TO MAKE UP

Press according to ball band. Darn in ends.

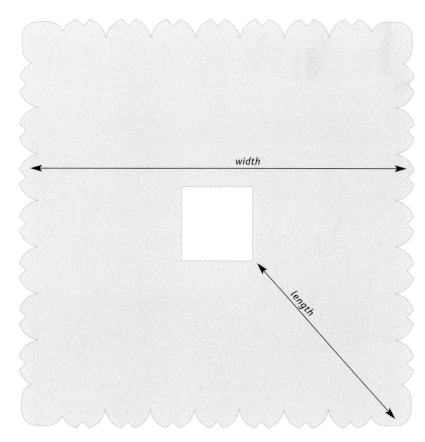

*Increasing and decreasing at regular intervals in treble crochet makes a zigzag pattern that is emphasized by brilliant colour changes.*

# LONG ZIGZAG SCARF

*You'll find it easy to follow the colour changes if you cut snippets of the yarn and stick them down in the order given on a spare piece of paper. This will allow you to see at a glance which colour to use next.*

*The scarf starts with a treble chain rather than the ordinary type of chain because a treble chain gives a more flexible edge and is a lot easier to work into for the first row.*

*The starting chain is a multiple of 16 plus 1, the pattern is a multiple of 17 plus 1.*

## HELPFUL HINTS

- If you don't want to do treble chain, you can work the same number of ordinary chain very loosely, plus three chain to count as first stitch, then work an extra row in A.
- When changing colours, work the last loop of the last stitch of the row in the next colour.
- Cut the yarn and work over the ends each time you change colours. Do not carry yarns up the side of the work, as they will show. Make sure that the worked over ends lie on top of stitches of the same colour. For single row stripes, weave the new end in as you work the 3 ch, then work over the tail of the yarn at the end of the next row.

## MEASUREMENTS

25.5 × 194 cm
10 × 86½ in

## MATERIALS

- 2 × 50 g balls of Patons Diploma Gold DK in each of the following: Berry 06129 (A), Hot Pink 06247 (B), Honey 06228 (D), Ginger 06211 (E) and Jaffa 06252 (F)
- 1 × 50 g ball of Patons Diploma Gold DK in Red 06151 (C)
- 4.00 mm crochet hook

## TENSION

17 sts measure 8.5 cm (3⅜ in), 9 rows to 10 cm (4 in) over chevron pattern using 4.00 mm hook. Change hook size if necessary to obtain this tension.

## ABBREVIATIONS

*See page 9.*

## SCARF

**Treble chain:** Using A, make a slip knot and work 3 ch, 1 tr in 3rd ch from hook, * inserting hook under two strands at bottom left of previous tr, work 1 tr in previous tr, rep from * until there are 49 sts.

**Row 1:** (RS) 3 ch, 1 tr in 1st tr, [1 tr in each of next 7 tr, miss 1 tr, 1 tr in each of next 7 tr, 3 tr in next tr] twice, 1 tr in each of next 7 tr, miss 1 tr, 1 tr in each of next 7 tr, 2 tr in last st. [52 sts.] Change to B.

**Row 2:** 3 ch, 1 tr in 1st tr, [1 tr in each of next 7 tr, miss 2 tr, 1 tr in each of next 7 tr, 3 tr in next tr] twice, 1 tr in each of next 7 tr, miss 2 tr, 1 tr in each of next 7 tr, 2 tr in last st.

Row 2 forms the chevron pattern.

Work 2 more rows B, 1 row A, 1 row B.

First 7-row repeat has been completed.

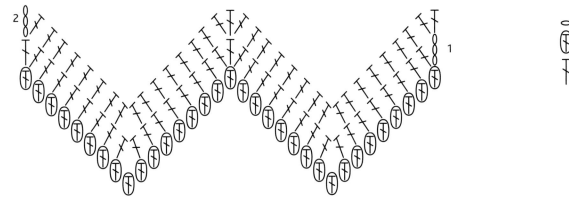

| | |
|---|---|
| $\circ$ | ch |
| $\oplus$ | trch |
| $\dagger$ | tr |

Work in stripe pattern as follows:
2 rows C, 3 rows D, 1 row C, 1 row D,
2 rows E, 3 rows F, 1 row E, 1 row F,
2 rows C, 3 rows A, 1 row C, 1 row A,
2 rows B, 3 rows F, 1 row B, 1 row F,
2 rows D, 3 rows E, 1 row D, 1 row E,
2 rows A, 3 rows B, 1 row A, 1 row B.
These 42 rows form the stripe patt.
Work last 42 rows 3 more times. Fasten off.

# VARIATION

### ONE-COLOUR SCARF

The chevron pattern will create an interesting texture if you make the scarf in just one colour. For a scarf the same size as the main project, you will need 7 × 50 g balls of Patons Diploma Gold DK.

*Using just two easy-to-work square motifs, the colour tones
in this gilet are mixed and matched to create a random effect.
Panels on each side of the gilet give it a shaped fit.*

# PATCHWORK SQUARES GILET

## HELPFUL HINTS
- This is an ideal project to carry around with you so you can work a square whenever you have a few spare moments.
- Raised stitches and popcorns add texture interest to the motifs.

## MEASUREMENTS
### To fit bust

| | | | |
|---|---|---|---|
| 81–86 | 91–97 | 102–107 | cm |
| 32–34 | 36–38 | 40–42 | in |

### Actual width

| | | | |
|---|---|---|---|
| 85 | 96 | 104 | cm |
| 33½ | 37¾ | 41 | in |

### Actual length
65 cm
25½ in

*In the instructions figures are given for the
smallest size first; larger sizes follow in
brackets. Where only one set of figures is
given this applies to all sizes.*

## MATERIALS
- 2 × 100 g balls of Sirdar Country Style DK in each of Parchment 404 (A), Chocolate 530 (B) and Cream 411 (C)
- 3 buttons
- 3.50 mm crochet hook

## TENSION
Each motif measures 8 cm (3⅛ in) square,
22 sts and 9 rows to 10 cm (4 in) over treble
crochet both using 3.50 mm hook. Change
hook size if necessary to obtain this tension.

## ABBREVIATIONS
**PC** – work 3tr in same st, remove hook from
working loop and insert in top of first tr,
pick up working loop, draw through and
work 1ch to close popcorn
**Rdtr** – take yarn twice around hook, insert
hook from right to left around stem of tr one
row below, yrh and draw loop through, [yrh
and pull through 2 loops] 3 times
**2trtog** – leaving last loop of each st on
hook, work 1tr in each of next 2 sts, yrh and
pull through 3 loops on hook
*See also page 9.*

## NOTE
Make 29 of each of the flower and square
motifs and one of each half motif.
A, B and C are given for the first square in
each motif, change colours to work five of
each motif in ABC, ACB, BAC, BCA, CAB
and four in CBA.

*After changing
colours, work over
the ends to save time
darning in.*

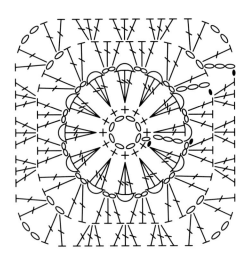
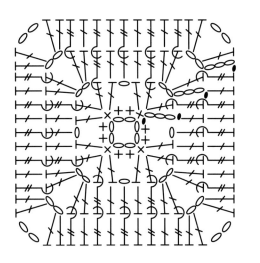
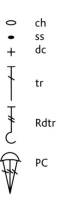

| | |
|---|---|
| ○ | ch |
| • | ss |
| + | dc |
| † | tr |
| ‡ | Rdtr |
| ⬥ | PC |

# GILET

### FLOWER MOTIF

Using A, make 8 ch, ss in 1st ch to form a ring.

**Round 1:** (RS) 1 ch, 12 dc in ring, ss in 1st dc.

**Round 2:** 3 ch, 2 tr in same place as ss, remove hook, insert in 3rd ch, pick up working loop, draw through and work 1 ch to close 1st popcorn, [2 ch, 1 PC in next dc] 11 times, 2 ch, ss in 1st PC. Fasten off. Join B in next 2 ch sp.

**Round 3:** 3 ch, 1 tr, 2 ch, 2 tr in first ch sp, [3 tr in each of next 2 ch sps, 2 tr, 2 ch, 2 tr in foll ch sp] 3 times, 3 tr in each of next 2 ch sps, ss in 3rd ch. Fasten off. Join C to a corner 2 ch sp.

**Round 4:** 3 ch, 1 tr, 2 ch, 2 tr in first ch sp, * [3 tr between next tr group] 3 times, 2 tr, 2 ch, 2 tr in next ch sp, rep from * two more times [3 tr between next tr group] 3 times, ss in 3rd ch. Fasten off.

### HALF FLOWER MOTIF

Using B, make 6 ch, ss in 1st ch to form a ring.

**Row 1:** (RS) 1 ch, 6 dc in ring. Fasten off. Join B to 1st dc.

**Row 2:** 4 ch, 1 PC in 1st dc, [2 ch, 1 PC in next dc] 5 times, 1 ch, 1 tr in last dc. Fasten off. Join C to 4 ch sp.

**Row 3:** 5 ch, 2 tr in same ch sp, [3 tr in next ch sp] twice, 2 tr, 2 ch, 2 tr in foll ch sp, [3 tr in next ch sp] twice, 2 tr, 2 ch, 1 tr in last ch sp. Fasten off. Join A in 5 ch sp.

**Row 4:** 5 ch, 2 tr in 5 ch sp, [3 tr between next tr group] 3 times, 2 tr, 2 ch, 2 tr in 2 ch sp, [3 tr between next tr group] 3 times, 2 tr, 2 ch, 1 tr in last ch sp. Fasten off.

### SQUARE MOTIF

Using A, make 8 ch, ss in 1st ch to form a ring.

**Round 1:** (RS) 1 ch, 12 dc in ring, ss in 1st dc.

**Round 2:** 3 ch, 1 tr, 2 ch, 2 tr in 1st dc, 1 ch, miss 2 dc, [2 tr, 2 ch, 2 tr in next dc, 1 ch, miss 2 dc] 3 times, ss in 3rd ch. Fasten off. Join B to a corner 2 ch sp.

**Round 3:** 3 ch, 1 tr, 2 ch, 2 tr in 1st 2 ch sp, [1 Rdtr in next tr, 1 tr in foll tr, 1 tr in ch sp, 1 tr in next tr, 1 Rdtr in foll tr, 2 tr, 2 ch, 2 tr in next 2 ch sp] 3 times, 1 Rdtr in next tr, 1 tr in foll tr, 1 tr in ch sp, 1 tr in next tr, 1 Rdtr in foll tr, ss in 3rd ch. Fasten off. Join C to a corner 2 ch sp.

**Round 4:** 3 ch, 1 tr, 2 ch, 2 tr in 1st 2 ch sp, * [1 Rdtr in next st, 1 tr in foll st] 4 times, 1 Rdtr in next st, 2 tr, 2 ch, 2 tr in 2 ch sp, rep from * 2 more times, [1 Rdtr in next st, 1 tr in foll st] 4 times, 1 Rdtr in next st, ss in 3rd ch. Fasten off.

## HALF SQUARE MOTIF

Using B, make 6 ch, ss in 1st ch to form a ring.

**Row 1:** (RS) 1 ch, 7 dc in ring. Fasten off. Join B to 1st dc.

**Row 2:** 5 ch, 2 tr in 1st dc, 1 ch, miss 2 dc, 2 tr, 2 ch, 2 tr in next dc, 1 ch, miss 2 dc, 2 tr, 2 ch, 1 tr in last dc. Fasten off. Join C to 5 ch sp.

**Row 3:** 5 ch, 2 tr in 5 ch sp, * 1 Rdtr in next tr, 1 tr in foll tr, 1 tr in ch sp, 1 tr in next tr, 1 Rdtr in foll tr *, 2 tr, 2 ch, 2 tr in 2 ch sp, rep from * to *, 2 tr, 2 ch, 1 tr in last ch sp. Fasten off. Join A in 5 ch sp.

**Row 4:** 5 ch, 2 tr in 5 ch sp, * [1 Rdtr in next st, 1 tr in foll st] 4 times, 1 Rdtr in next st *, 2 tr, 2 ch, 2 tr in 2 ch sp, rep from * to *, 2 tr, 2 ch, 1 tr in last 2 ch sp. Fasten off.

## SIDE PANELS

Using B, make 27 (35:43) ch.

**Row 1:** (RS) 1 tr in 4th ch from hook, 1 tr in each tr to end. [25 (33:41) sts.]

**Row 2:** 3 ch, miss 1st tr, 1 tr in each tr to last st, 1 tr in 3rd ch.

Row 2 forms treble crochet. Cont in tr, work 2 more rows. Place a marker at each side of centre 5 tr.

**Dec row:** (RS) 3 ch, miss 1st tr, 1 tr in each tr to 2 tr from 1st marker, 2trtog, slip marker, 1 tr in each of next 5 tr, slip marker, 2trtog, 1 tr in each st to end.

*length*

[23 (31:39) sts.] Decrease in this way at each side of centre 5 tr on next 3 RS rows. [17 (25:33) sts.] Work 3 rows.

**Inc row:** (RS) 3 ch, miss 1st tr, 1 tr in each tr to 1 tr from 1st marker, 2 tr in next tr, slip marker, 1 tr in each of next 5 tr, slip marker, 2 tr in next tr, 1 tr in each st to end. [19 (27:35) sts.] Cont in tr, inc in this way at each side of centre 5 tr on 4 foll 4th rows. [27 (35:43) sts.] Patt 5 rows.

### Shape armholes

**Row 1:** 3 ch, miss 1st tr, 1 tr in each of next 3 tr, 2trtog, 1 tr in next tr, turn and complete first side on these 6 sts.

**Row 2:** 3 ch, 2trtog, 1 tr in each of next 3 sts. [5 sts.]

**Row 3:** 3 ch, miss 1st tr, 1 tr in next tr, 2trtog, 1 tr in 3rd ch. [4 sts.]

**Row 4:** 3 ch, miss 1st tr, 2trtog, 1 tr in 3rd ch. [3 sts.] Fasten off. Miss centre 13 (21:29) tr, join yarn in next tr and work second side to match.

### TO MAKE UP

**To join two motifs:** Using A, join yarn in corner 2 ch sp of a motif. With WS together and taking hook through one st from each motif each time, work 1 dc in corner sps, 1 dc in each st along edge, 1 dc in corner sps. Fasten off.

Alternating flower and square motifs and placing different colourway motifs at random, join squares to make 6 strips of 8 motifs and 2 strips of 5 motifs. With diagonal edge towards neck edge, join one half square at top of each of the 5-motif strips. Working dc in same way as before along all squares, join four 8-square strips to form back and one 8-square strip and one 5½-square strip for each front.

With shaped points at underarm ending level with the centre of the 6th square, using A and dc, join side panels to front and back edges. Using A, backstitch over the line of dc to make it lie flat.

**Armhole edgings:** With RS facing, join A to centre st at underarm and work 1 round dc around armhole, ss in 1st dc. Fasten off. With WS facing, join C and work 3 rounds dc. Fasten off.

**Front, neck and lower edging:** With RS facing, join A to left back seam, work 1 round dc all around edge, ss in 1st dc. Fasten off. With WS facing, join C, work 2 rounds dc, working extra sts and skipping sts as necessary to keep edging flat.

**Buttonhole round:** Work in dc until level with join between half motif and top square of right front, [3 ch, miss 3 dc, 1 dc in each of next 11 dc] twice, 3 ch, miss 3 dc, cont in dc to end. Working 3 dc in each 3 ch sp, work 1 more round dc. Fasten off. Sew on buttons.

Made mostly in double crochet, this jacket is very simple to work. The exquisitely shaded colours in the pure wool, hand-spun effect yarn add interest to the simple stitch pattern.

# ZIP-UP JACKET

## HELPFUL HINTS

- Check the front length before buying the zip. If the zip is longer than needed, fold the top ends under and secure, then hide the ends inside the collar.

## MEASUREMENTS

### To fit bust

| | | | | | | |
|---|---|---|---|---|---|---|
| 81 | 86 | 91 | 97 | 102 | 107 | cm |
| 32 | 34 | 36 | 38 | 40 | 42 | in |

### Actual width

| | | | | | | |
|---|---|---|---|---|---|---|
| 92.5 | 97 | 101.5 | 106 | 110.5 | 115 | cm |
| 36½ | 38 | 40 | 41¾ | 43½ | 45¼ | in |

### Actual length

| | | | | | | |
|---|---|---|---|---|---|---|
| 48.5 | 50 | 51 | 52 | 54 | 54.5 | cm |
| 19 | 19½ | 20 | 20½ | 21¼ | 21½ | in |

### Actual sleeve

| | | | | | | |
|---|---|---|---|---|---|---|
| 46 | 47 | 47 | 47 | 48 | 48 | cm |
| 18 | 18½ | 18½ | 18½ | 19 | 19 | in |

*In the instructions figures are given for the smallest size first; larger sizes follow in brackets. Where only one set of figures is given this applies to all sizes.*

## MATERIALS

- 11 (12:13:14:15:16) × 50 g balls of Noro Kureyon 139
- 5.00 mm crochet hook
- 50 (50:55:55:55:55) cm (20 (20:22:22:22:22) in) open-ended zip

## TENSION

15 sts and 18 rows to 10 cm (4 in) measured over double crochet using 5.00 mm hook. Change hook size if necessary to obtain this tension.

## ABBREVIATIONS

**2dctog** – leaving loop on hook each time, ss in each of next 2 sts, yrh and pull though 3 loops on hook
*See also page 9.*

# JACKET

The body of the jacket is worked in one from front to front so the rows run the length of the garment and the shaded yarn makes vertical stripes.

## Left front

Make 61 (61:63:64:67:68) ch.
**Row 1:** 1 dc in 2nd ch from hook, 1 dc in each ch to end. [60 (60:62:63:66:67) sts.]
**Row 2:** (RS) 1ch, 1 dc in each dc to end. 2nd row forms double crochet.
Cont in dc, work 9 (11:11:11:11:13) more rows.

## Shape neck

**Inc row:** (RS) 1 ch, 1 dc in each dc to last dc, 2 dc in last dc.
Cont in dc, inc in this way at end of next

3 RS rows. [64 (64:66:67:70:71) sts.] At end of last row, make 10 (12:12:12:12:12) ch, turn.

## Shape shoulder

**Next row:** (WS) 1 dc in 2nd ch from hook, 1 dc in each dc to end.
[73 (75:77:78:81:82) sts.] Cont in dc, work 12 (12:14:16:18:18) rows.

## Shape side and left armhole

** **Row 1:** (RS) 1 ch, 1 dc in each of next 10 dc, ss in each of next 15 dc, 1 dc in each dc to end.

**Row 2:** 1 ch, 1 dc in each of next 48 (50:52:53:56:57) dc, 1 dc in each of next 15 ss, 1 dc in each of next 10 dc.

**Row 3:** 1 ch, 1 dc in each of next 10 dc, ss in each of next 15 dc, 1 dc in each of next 26 (26:27:27:28:28) dc, turn.

**Rows 4, 6 and 8:** 1 ch, miss 1st dc, 1 dc in each dc to ss, 1 dc in each ss, 1 dc in each dc to end.

**Row 5:** 1 ch, 1 dc in each of next 10 dc, ss in each of next 15 dc, 1 dc in each of next 24 (24:25:25:26:26) dc, turn.

**Row 7:** 1 ch, 1 dc in each of next 10 dc, ss in each of next 15 dc, 1 dc in each of next 22 (22:23:23:24:24) dc, turn.

**Row 9:** 1 ch, 1 dc in each of next 10 dc, ss in each of next 15 dc, 1 dc in each of next 20 (20:21:21:22:22) dc, turn.

[45 (45:46:46:47:47) sts.]
Shaping by working ss in same way as before, work 4 rows.

**Rows 14, 16 and 18:** 1 ch, 2 dc in 1st dc, 1 dc in each st to end.

**Rows 15, 17 and 19:** 1 ch, 1 dc in each of next 10 dc, ss in each of next 15 dc, 1 dc in each dc to last dc, 2 dc in last dc.

[51 (51:52:52:53:53) sts.] At end of last row, make 23 (25:26:27:29:30) ch, turn.

## Shape back

**Row 1:** (WS) 1 dc in 2nd ch from hook, 1 dc in each st to end.

**Row 2:** 1 ch, 1 dc in each of next 10 dc, ss in each of next 15 dc, 1 dc in each dc to end. [73 (75:77:78:81:82) sts **.]
Cont in dc, work 63 (67:71:75:79:83) rows.

## Shape side and right armhole

Work as given for shape side and left armhole from ** to **.

## Shape shoulder

Cont in dc, work 13 (13:15:17:19:19) rows.

## Shape neck

**Row 1:** (RS) 1 ch, 1 dc in each dc to last 9 (11:11:11:11:11) dc, turn.
[64 (64:66:67:70:71) sts.]
**Dec row:** (WS) 1 ch, miss 1 st dc, 1 dc in each dc to end.

Cont in dc, dec in this way at beg of next 3 WS rows. [60 (60:62:63:66:67) sts.] Cont in dc, work 10 (12:12:12:12:14) rows. Fasten off.

## SLEEVES (MAKE 2)
Make 34 (34:36:36:38:38) ch.
**Row 1:** (WS) 1 dc in 2nd ch from hook, 1 dc in each ch to end.
[33 (33:35:35:37:37) sts.]
**Row 2:** (RS) 1 ch, 1 dc in each dc to end. Row 2 forms double crochet.
Work 15 (13:13:13:9:3) more rows dc.
**Inc row:** (RS) 1 ch, 1 dc in 1st dc, 2 dc in next dc, 1 dc in each dc to last 2 dc, 2 dc in next dc, 1 dc in last dc.
[35 (35:37:37:39:39) sts.]
Cont in dc, inc in this way at each end of 7 (8:10:11:12:13) foll 8th (8th:6th:6th:6th:6th) rows. [49 (51:57:59:63:65) sts.]
Work 9 (5:9:3:3:3) rows.

### Shape top
**Next row:** (RS) Ss in each of first 3 dc, 1 ch, 1 dc in each dc to last 3 dc, turn.
[43 (45:51:53:57:59) sts.]
**Dec row:** 1 ch, miss 1st dc, 1 dc in each dc to last 2 dc, 2dctog.
[41 (43:49:51:55:57) sts.]
Cont in dc, dec in this way at each end of next 13 (14:16:17:19:20) rows.
[15 (15:17:17:17:17) sts.] Fasten off.

## COLLAR
Matching sts, join shoulders.
**Row 1:** (RS) Join yarn 2 rows in from right front edge, work 23 (24:24:24:24:25) ss up right front neck, 24 (26:26:26:26:28) ss across back neck and 23 (24:24:24:24:25) ss down left front neck to last 2 rows.
[70 (74:74:74:74:78) sts.]
**Row 2:** 1 ch, 1 dc in each ss to end.
**Row 3:** 1 ch, 1 dc in each dc to end.
Row 3 forms double crochet. Work 1 more row dc.
**Dec row:** (RS) 1 ch, 1 dc in each of first 2 dc, [2dctog, 1 dc in each of next 2 dc] to end. [53 (56:56:56:56:59) sts.]
Cont in dc until collar measures 15 cm (6 in), ending with a WS row.
**Inc row:** (RS) 1 ch, 1 dc in each of first 2 dc, [2 dc in next dc, 1 dc in each of next 2 dc] to end. [70 (74:74:74:74:78) sts.]
Work 2 rows dc. Fasten off.
**Edgings:** With RS facing, join yarn and work 28 ss across row-ends of collar, turn and work 1 ch, 1 dc in each ss to end. Fasten off. Work other side to match.

## TO MAKE UP
Press according to ball band. Mark centre of collar at each front edge. Set in zip, ending at markers. Fold collar in half to WS, sew edgings to zip, then slipstitch last row of collar to neck edge. Join sleeve

## SETTING A ZIP IN A CROCHET GARMENT

Make sure the zip opens and closes properly, then lay the zip on a flat surface with the RS of zip and jacket facing. Slip the zip fabric under the front edges. Setting the zip at right angles to the edge, pin in place using long pins. Check that the stitches along each edge of the jacket line up, and that the crochet fabric and zip are lying flat. Tack the zip in place. Remove the pins, open the zip and turn the jacket inside out. Slipstitch the edge of the zip fabric in place. Follow the same line of crochet stitches up the front so the edges are straight. Do up the zip again to check that both sides match. Undo the zip and with RS facing, backstitch through the crochet fabric and zip as near to the teeth as possible, removing the tacking thread as you sew. Keep the needle vertical and work one stitch at a time, stitching in a stabbing motion. Don't scoop through the layers or they may slip and become bumpy.

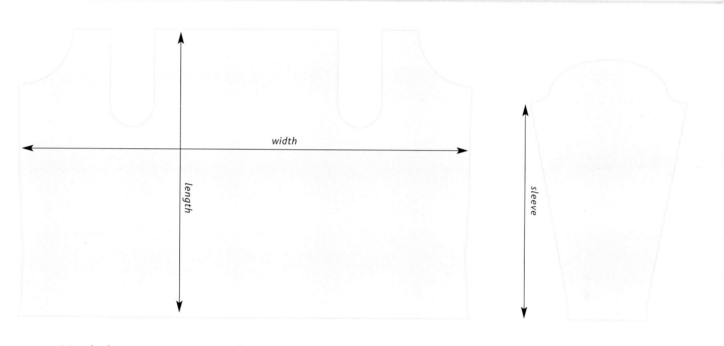

seams. Match sleeve seam to centre of underarm and shoulder seam to centre top of sleeve, then, easing to fit, set in sleeves.

# VARIATION

### ZIP-UP GILET

To make a zip-up gilet, simply omit the sleeves and neaten the armhole edges with a few rounds of dc.
You will need around 7 (8:8:9:10:11) × 50 g balls of Noro Kureyon.

*Made using just one hank of yarn, this wild and woolly scarf does double duty in keeping you both warm and fashionable during the cold winter months.*

# LOOPY STITCH BOA

*Make the starting chain loosely. If necessary, use a hook that is a size larger than stated in the pattern.*

## HELPFUL HINTS

- Loop stitch is really just a double crochet with the middle strand of yarn elongated. It is worked on wrong side rows so that the loops show on the right side.

## MEASUREMENTS

4.5 × 134 cm
1¾ × 53 in

## MATERIALS

- 1 × 100 g hank of Debbie Bliss Maya in red 10
- 7.00 mm crochet hook

## TENSION

8½ sts to 10 cm (4 in), 6 rows measure 4.5 cm (1¾ in) over loop stitch patt using 7.00 mm hook. Change hook size if necessary to obtain this tension.

## ABBREVIATIONS

**Lp1** – insert hook, extend middle finger to form a loop, catch back and front strands of the loop of yarn with hook and pull through to make 3 loops on hook, take hook to left of long loop on finger, yarn around hook and pull through to secure the 3 loops, remove finger.
*See also page 9.*

## BOA

Make 115 ch.
**Row 1:** Lp1 in 2nd ch from hook, work Lp1 in each ch to end. [114 sts.]
**Row 2:** (WS). 1 ch, work Lp1 in each st to end.
**Row 3:** 1 ch, work 1 dc in each st to end.
Rows 2 and 3 form loop st patt.
Patt 3 more rows. Fasten off.
Steam lightly on WS. Darn in ends.

# WEEKEND

From town chic to country casual you can relax and unwind in style with these fabulous makes. If you want something you can crochet and wear in the same weekend, choose a wonderful, fast-working project like the chunky beret or the flower and mesh scarf. If you're out and about, wrap up in the figure-skimming, shaded coat in a lightweight, textured yarn. Brighten up a dull day or a dull outfit with the tassel-edged wrap in a stunning colour. And if your weekend starts on a Friday night, make the flower motifs long cardigan for the ultimate in office-hours-to-happy-hour style.

# CHUNKY BLUE BERET

*Check that your starting chain will fit around your head, if it is too tight, redo it working more loosely.*

*Do not count the 1 ch at the start of double crochet rounds as a stitch, simply ss in the first dc, then on the next round, work the first dc in the same dc as the ss of the previous round.*

*Count the 3 ch at the start of treble rounds as a stitch.*

*2 ch and 1 tr at the start of the round is the equivalent of 2trtog.*

*Work the 3rd ch at the start of treble rounds loosely, this will make it easier to insert the hook under both loops of the 3rd ch to work the ss at the end to join the round.*

*There are just nine rounds from start to finish, so making this flattering hat could take as little as two hours.*

## HELPFUL HINTS

- The beret is worked in the round so there is no sewing up, just darn in the ends and it's ready to wear.

## MEASUREMENTS

Actual measurement round head

58 cm

23 in

## MATERIALS

- 2 × 100 g balls of Sirdar Bigga in Delta Blue 688
- 9.00 mm crochet hook

## TENSION

5½ sts and 3 rows to 10 cm (4 in) measured over treble crochet using 9.00 mm hook. Change hook size if necessary to obtain this tension.

## ABBREVIATIONS

**2dctog** – insert hook in next st, yrh and pull loop through, insert hook in foll st, yrh and pull loop through, yrh and pull through 3 loops on hook

**2trtog** – leaving last loop of each st on hook, work 1tr in each of next 2 sts, yrh and pull through 3 loops on hook
*See also page 9.*

## BERET

Leaving a 15-cm (6-in) end, make 33 ch.

**Round 1:** 1 dc in 2nd ch from hook, 1 dc in each ch to end, turn and ss in 1st st to join in a round. [32 sts.]

**Rounds 2 and 3:** (RS) 1 ch, 1 dc in each dc to end, ss in 1st dc.

**Round 4:** 3 ch, 1 tr in same dc as ss, 1 tr in each of next 2 dc, [2 tr in each of next 2 dc, 1 tr in each of foll 2 dc] 7 times, 2 tr in last dc, ss in 3rd ch. [48 sts.]

**Round 5:** 3 ch, 1 tr in each tr to end, ss in 3rd ch.

**Round 6:** 2 ch, 1 tr in each of next 3 tr, * [2trtog] twice, 1 tr in each of next 2 tr, rep from * 6 more times, 2trtog, ss in 1st tr. [32 sts.]

**Round 7:** 2 ch, 1 tr in next tr, [2trtog] 15 times, ss in 1st tr. [16 sts.]

**Round 8:** 2 ch, 1 tr in next tr, [2trtog] 7 times, ss in 1st tr. [8 sts.]

**Round 9:** [2dctog] 4 times, ss in 1st st. [4 sts.] Leaving a 15-cm (6-in) end, fasten off.

## TO MAKE UP

Thread end through front loop of each st of Round 9, draw up and secure. Darn in ends at start of 2nd ball of yarn. Join 1st and last sts of Round 1 while darning end at beginning of Round 1.

*This beautiful hot pink scarf is incredibly quick to crochet – just eleven rows to do and you're ready to wrap up and keep warm.*

# FLOWER AND MESH PATTERNED SCARF

## MEASUREMENTS
**Actual width**
23 cm
9 in
**Actual length (including tassels)**
260 cm
102 in

## MATERIALS
- 4 × 100 g balls of Rowan Big Wool in Whoosh 14
- 9.00 mm crochet hook

## TENSION
16 sts (two repeats) measure 30 cm (12 in). 5 rows to 10 cm (4 in) measured over flower and mesh pattern using 9.00 mm hook. Change hook size if necessary to obtain this tension.

## ABBREVIATIONS
**2trcl** – leaving last loop of each st on hook, work 2 tr in stitch indicated, yrh and pull through 3 loops on hook
*See also page 9.*

## SCARF

Make a slip knot and work 2 ch, 1 dc in 2nd ch from hook, * inserting hook under two strands at bottom left of previous dc, work 1 dc in previous dc, rep from * until there are 117 sts.

**Row 1:** (WS) 1 ch, 1 dc in each dc to end.
**Row 2:** 1 ch, 1 dc in 1st dc, 3 ch, 2 trcl in dc at beg, miss 3 dc, 2 trcl in next dc, 3 ch, ss in same dc, [6 ch, miss 3 dc, ss in next dc, 3 ch, 2 trcl in same dc, miss 3 dc, 2 trcl in next dc, 3 ch, ss in same dc] 14 times.
**Row 3:** 5 ch, 2 trcl in top of first 2 trcl, 3 ch, ss in same 2 trcl, 3 ch, 2 trcl in same 2 trcl, [3 ch, 1 dc in 6 ch sp, 3 ch, 2 trcl in top of next 2 trcl, 3 ch, ss in same 2 trcl, 3 ch, 2 trcl in same 2 trcl] 14 times, 1 trtr in last dc.
**Row 4:** 1 ch, 1 dc in trtr, [3 ch, 1 dc in top of next 2 trcl] to end.
**Row 5:** 1 ch, 1 dc in 1st dc, [3 dc in 3 ch sp, 1 dc in next dc] to end.
**Row 6:** 1 ch, 1 dc in each dc to end.
**Row 7:** As row 2.
**Row 8:** As row 3.
**Row 9:** As row 4.
**Row 10:** As row 5.
**Row 11:** As row 6.
Fasten off.

## TO MAKE UP
Join yarn and work 16 dc across one short edge. Work 2 more rows dc. Fasten off. Finish the other short edge in the same way. Using ten 42 cm (16½ in) lengths of yarn for each tassel, make 10 tassels. Sew 5 tassels on each short edge. Press according to instructions on ball band. Trim tassels.

*Starting with a dc chain gives a more flexible edge. A dc chain is also easier to count than ordinary chain.*

*Work the 3 ch on the 4th row loosely so the row doesn't pull in.*

*When working into top of 2 trcl, lift the loose strand below with the hook and work into this strand and the front loop of the stitch.*

| | |
|---|---|
| ○ | ch |
| • | ss |
| + | dc |
| ⊕ | dcch |
| Ⓝ | 2trcl |
| ┬ | trtr |

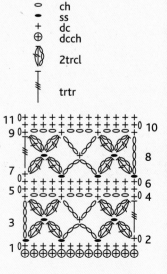

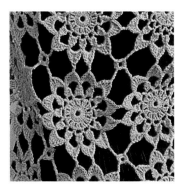

*Big flower wheel motifs in 4-ply cotton are joined together in rows to make this dramatic long cardigan. A subtle realignment of the motifs at the underarm gives a slender line to the sleeve top.*

# LACY MOTIFS LONG CARDIGAN

★★★ MEDIUM

🖐 *The second size has the same number of motifs joined in the same way as the first size but the motifs are worked on a bigger hook to make them larger. Tensions can vary a lot in crochet and as the size of the cardigan depends on the size of each flower motif, do check your tension carefully. If your motif is too big, try again using a smaller hook, if it is too small, try again using a larger hook.*

🖐 *This motif uses several different height stitches to make the outer petals. Here's a reminder of how many times to take the yarn around the hook at the start of each stitch: dc = no times, htr = once but pull through all first time; tr = once; dtr = twice, trtr = 3 times.*

## HELPFUL HINTS

- 4-ply cotton can be slippery, if you need to increase the tension on the supply yarn, take it around the little finger in the usual way, then over and around the middle finger as well.
- To make a neat centre for the flower motif, wind the yarn around first finger of left hand, insert hook, yrh and pull through. Work over end as well as into ring, then before joining Round 1 pull the end to tighten the ring. Darn in end securely before trimming it off.
- Instructions are given for joining lines of flower motifs, then working a line of filler motifs but you could work fillers each time there's a space.

## MEASUREMENTS
### To fit bust

| | | |
|---|---|---|
| 81–91 | 97–107 | cm |
| 32–36 | 38–42 | in |

### Actual width

| | | |
|---|---|---|
| 92 | 108 | cm |
| 36 | 42½ | in |

### Actual length

| | | |
|---|---|---|
| 80.5 | 94.5 | cm |
| 31½ | 37 | in |

### Actual sleeve

| | | |
|---|---|---|
| 46 | 54 | cm |
| 18 | 21¼ | in |

*In the instructions figures are given for the smaller size first; larger size follows in brackets. Where only one set of figures is given this applies to both sizes.*

## MATERIALS

- 5 (6) × 100 g balls of Patons 100% Cotton 4-ply in Ocean 01711
- 2.00 (3.00) mm crochet hook

## TENSION

One flower motif measures 11.5 (13.5) cm (4½ (5¼) in) across when pressed, using 2.00 (3.00) mm hook. Change hook size if necessary to obtain these tensions.

## ABBREVIATIONS

**4dtrcl** – leaving last loop of each st on hook, work 4dtr, yrh and pull through all 5 loops on hook
*See also page 9.*

# CARDIGAN
## BACK AND FRONTS

**1st line of flower motifs**
**1st motif:** Wind yarn around finger to form a ring.

**Round 1:** (RS) 3 ch, work 23 tr in ring, pull end to tighten ring, ss in 3rd ch. [24 sts.]

**Round 2:** 3 ch, 1 tr in same place as ss, 1 ch, miss 1 tr, [2 tr in next tr, 1 ch, miss 1 tr] 11 times, 1 ch, ss in 3rd ch.

**Round 3:** Ss in 1st tr, 1 dc in 1st 1 ch sp, 5 ch, [1 dc in next 1 ch sp, 5 ch] 11 times, ss in 1st dc.

**Round 4:** Ss in each of first 3 ch, 4 ch, leaving last loop of each st on hook, work 3 dtr in ch sp, yrh and pull through all 4 loops on hook to make first 4dtrcl, [7 ch, 4dtrcl in next 5 ch sp] 11 times, 7 ch, ss in 1st dtrcl.

**Round 5:** [1 dc, 1 htr, 1 tr, 2 dtr, 2 ch, 2 dtr, 1 tr, 1 htr, 1 dc in next 7 ch sp] 12 times, ss in 1st dc. Fasten off.

## 2nd and following motifs

Work as given for 1st motif until Round 4 has been completed.

**Round 5:** [1 dc, 1 htr, 1 tr, 2 dtr, 2 ch, 2 dtr, 1 tr, 1 htr, 1 dc in next 7 ch sp] 10 times, in next 7 ch sp, work *1 dc, 1 htr, 1 tr, 2 dtr, 1 ch, with WS together, join with a tr in a 2 ch sp of 1st motif, 2 dtr, 1 tr, 1 htr, 1 dc, rep from * in next 7 ch sp joining to next 2 ch sp of 1st motif, ss in 1st dc. Fasten off.

Make 6 more motifs, joining motifs in the same way. Lay the line of motifs flat. The 1st and 2nd motifs on the left are the left front, the next 4 motifs are the back, and the last 2 motifs are the right front.

## 2nd line of flower motifs

**1st motif:** Work as given for 1st motif of first line of flower motifs until Round 4 has been completed. Work Round 5 until 10 petals have been completed, then join 11th and 12th petals to top two petals of 1st motif of left front.

**2nd motif:** Work as 1st motif until 7 petals have been completed. Join 8th and 9th petals to 1st motif of 2nd line, work one petal, join 11th and 12th petals to top two petals of 2nd motif of 1st line, so leaving 4 petals free at centre of join.

Make 6 more motifs joining in same way as 2nd motif.

**Filler motif:** Each filler motif is worked in the four petals free between lines of flower motifs. Make 8 ch, ss in 1st ch to form a ring.

**Round 1:** With WS together each time, work 1 trtr in 2 ch sp of 1st motif, 3 dc in ring, [1 trtr in 2 ch sp of next motif, 3 dc in ring] 3 times, ss in 1st trtr.

Fasten off. Work a filler motif in each of the remaining 6 spaces.

### 3rd 4th and 5th lines of flower motifs:

Work and join motifs in the same way as 2nd line of flower motifs, working filler motifs between each line of motifs.

## Divide for armhole

**6th line of flower motifs:** Work and join 1st and 2nd motifs. Omitting join between 2nd

*Keep a slim blunt-pointed needle handy and darn in ends as you work, then all you need to do is press your cardigan before you wear it.*

*Spray lightly with starch before pressing.*

and 3rd motifs for left armhole, join 3rd motif to 3rd motif of 5th line of flower motifs, then join 4th, 5th and 6th motifs in the usual way. Omitting join between 6th and 7th motifs for right armhole, join 7th motif to 7th motif of 5th line of flower motifs, then join 8th motif in the usual way. Work filler motifs between 5th and 6th lines of motifs.

### Shape neck

One motif is omitted at each end of 7th line and front and back motifs are joined at shoulders

### 7th line of motifs

**1st motif:** Join to 2nd motif of 6th line of flower motifs.

**2nd motif:** Work until 4 petals of Round 5 have been completed. Join 5th and 6th petals to top two petals of 1st motif of 7th line, work 4 petals, join 11th and 12th petals to top two petals of 3rd motif of 6th line of flower motifs.

**3rd, 4th and 5th motifs:** Join in the usual way.

**6th motif:** Work until 4 petals of Round 5 have been completed. Join 5th and 6th petals to top two petals of 5th motif of 7th line, work 4 petals, join 11th and 12th petals to top two petals of 7th motif of 6th line of flower motifs. Work a filler motif in each of the 3 spaces between the four motifs of the back, then work a triangle filler motif between three adjacent petals at each side of front neck.

### Triangle filler motif

Make 8 ch, ss in 1st ch to form a ring.
**Round 1:** With WS together each time, work 1 trtr in 2 ch sp of 1st motif, 3 dc in ring, [1 trtr in 2 ch sp of next motif, 3 dc in ring] twice, ss in 1st trtr.

### Join petals at neck edge

Leave two petals following triangle filler at neck edge of 6th motif of 7th line and join yarn in last petal. Work 10 ch, 1 dc in next petal of 5th motif of 7th line, 10 ch, ss in next petal of 4th motif of 7th line. Fasten off. Leave next 2 petals of 4th motif of 7th line and join yarn in last petal. Work 10 ch, ss in next petal of 3rd motif of 7th line. Fasten off. Leave next 2 petals of 3rd motif of 7th line and join yarn in last petal. 10 ch, 1 dc in next petal of 2nd motif of 7th line, 10 ch, ss in next petal of 1st motif of 7th line. Fasten off.

## LEFT SLEEVE

### 1st line of motifs

The 1st motif is placed at the underarm and joins four petals consecutively at the underarm.

**1st motif:** Work until 8 petals of Round 5 have been completed. Miss one petal of 2nd motif of 6th line, join 9th and 10th petals to remaining 2 petals of 2nd motif of 6th line, then join 11th and 12th petals to next 2 petals of 3rd motif of 6th line.

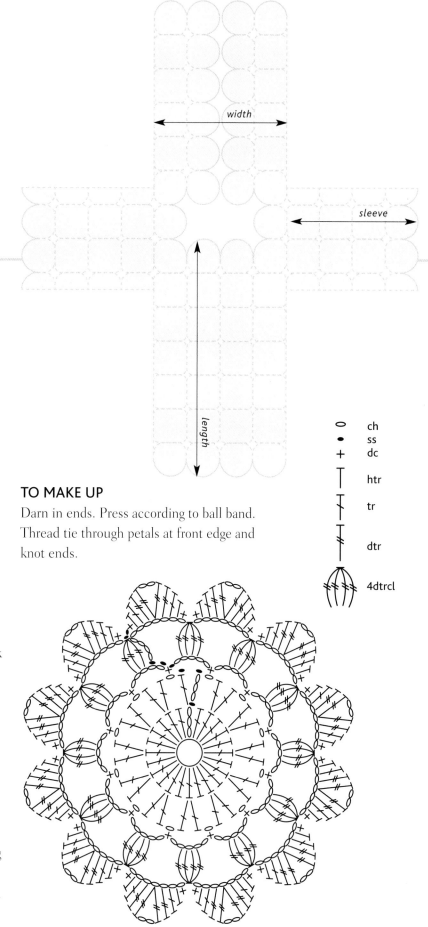

*Dotted lines on the diagram indicate joined motifs.*

**2nd motif:** Work until 7 petals of Round 5 have been completed. Join 8th and 9th petals to centre two petals of 1st motif of 7th line, work one petal, join 11th and 12th petals to next 2 petals of 1st sleeve motif.

**3rd motif:** Work until 4 petals of Round 5 have been completed, miss 4 petals and join 5th and 6th petals in last 2 petals of 1st sleeve motif, work one petal, miss one petal and join 8th and 9th petals in next 2 petals of 2nd motif of 7th line, work one petal, miss one petal and join 11th and 12th petals in next 2 petals of 2nd motif of 1st line of sleeve. Work a filler motif in the 4-petal space on the shoulder and a triangle filler motif in each 3-peal space at each side.

### 2nd, 3rd and 4th lines of motifs

Join 3 motifs in a round for each line and work filler motifs between.

### RIGHT SLEEVE

Work as left sleeve but joining 1st motif into 6th and 7th motifs of 6th line at underarm, 2nd motif into 5th motif of 7th line and 3rd motif into 6th motif of 7th line of motifs.

### TIE

Make 2 ch, 1 dc in 2nd ch from hook, working under 2 strands at side of dc each time, * work 1 dc in previous dc, repeat from * until tie measures 55 cm (21½ in). Fasten off.

### TO MAKE UP

Darn in ends. Press according to ball band. Thread tie through petals at front edge and knot ends.

| | |
|---|---|
| ○ | ch |
| ● | ss |
| + | dc |
| | htr |
| | tr |
| | dtr |
| | 4dtrcl |

*Worked mostly in treble crochet, this wrap over coat is designed to exploit the clever shaded effect of the lightweight bouclé yarn.*

# SHADED BLANKET COAT

✋ *Although this is a textured yarn, it's easy to crochet with because the bouclé loops are too small and closely spaced to catch on the hook.*

✋ *The back and fronts of the coat are worked in one to the armholes so the shading in the yarn flows around the body. The shading on the sleeves is wider than the colour stripes on the body because the rows are shorter.*

✋ *Use left over yarn to make a scarf. Simply make picots until the scarf is the width you want, then work in treble until the scarf is the length you want and finish off the edges with picots.*

## HELPFUL HINTS

- The picot edging is not just decorative, in this yarn it is easier to work into and between picots than to find the loops of a starting chain.
- When working the two rows to divide the back and fronts and shape the underarms, it's important to break and rejoin the yarn for each section to keep the continuity of the colour shading.

## MEASUREMENTS
### To fit bust
| | | | | |
|---|---|---|---|---|
| 81–86 | 91–97 | 102–107 | 112–117 | cm |
| 32–34 | 36–38 | 40–42 | 44–46 | in |

### Actual width
| | | | | |
|---|---|---|---|---|
| 89 | 100 | 110.5 | 121.5 | cm |
| 35 | 39¼ | 43½ | 47¾ | in |

### Actual length
| | | | | |
|---|---|---|---|---|
| 80 | 81.5 | 83 | 85 | cm |
| 31½ | 32 | 32¾ | 33½ | in |

### Actual sleeve seam
48 cm
19 in

*In the instructions figures are given for the smallest size first; larger sizes follow in brackets. Where only one set of figures is given this applies to all sizes.*

## MATERIALS
- 2 × 400 g balls of Sirdar Yo-Yo in Damson Mist 14
- 5.00 mm crochet hook

## TENSION
11 sts and 6 rows to 10 cm (4 in) measured over treble stitch using 5.00 mm hook. Change hook size if necessary to obtain this tension.

## ABBREVIATIONS
**2trtog** – leaving last loop of each st on hook, work a treble in each of next 2 sts, yrh and pull through 3 loops on hook
*See also page 9.*

## COAT
### BACK AND FRONTS
**Row 1:** 3 ch, 1 dc in 1st ch, [4 ch, 1 dc in 3rd ch] 72 (78:84:90) times.
**Row 2:** (WS) 1 dc in 1st picot, 2 ch, [1 tr between picots, 1 tr in next picot] 72 (78:84:90) times. [145 (157:169:181) sts.]
**Row 3:** 1 dc in 1st tr, 2 ch, 1 tr in each tr to last st, 1 tr in 2nd ch.
Row 3 forms treble crochet. Cont in tr, work 17 more rows.
**Dec row 1:** (RS) 1 dc in 1st tr, 2 ch, 1 tr in each of next 33 (36:39:42) tr, [2trtog] 4 times, 1 tr in each of next 61 (67:73:79) tr, [2trtog]

4 times, 1 tr in each of next 33 (36:39:42) tr, 1 tr in 2nd ch. [137 (149:161:173) sts.]
Cont in tr, work 3 rows.

**Dec row 2:** 1 dc in 1st tr, 2 ch, 1 tr in each of next 31 (34:37:40) tr, [2trtog] 4 times, 1 tr in each of next 57 (63:69:75) tr, [2trtog] 4 times, 1 tr in each of next 31 (34:37:40) tr, 1 tr in 2nd ch. [129 (141:153:165) sts.]
Cont in tr, work 3 rows.

**Dec row 3:** 1 dc in 1st tr, 2 ch, 1 tr in each of next 29 (32:35:38) tr, [2trtog] 4 times, 1 tr in each of next 53 (59:65:71) tr, [2trtog] 4 times, 1 tr in each of next 29 (32:35:38) tr, 1 tr in 2nd ch. [121 (133:145:157) sts.]
Cont in tr, work 3 rows.

**Dec row 4:** 1 dc in 1st tr, 2 ch, 1 tr in each of next 27 (30:33:36) tr, [2trtog] 4 times, 1 tr in each of next 49 (55:61:67) tr, [2trtog] 4 times, 1 tr in each of next 27 (30:33:36) tr, 1 tr in 2nd ch. [113 (125:137:149) sts.]
Cont in tr, work 3 rows.

**Dec row 5:** 1 dc in 1st tr, 2 ch, 1 tr in each of next 25 (28:31:34) tr, [2trtog] 4 times, 1 tr in each of next 45 (51:57:63) tr, [2trtog] 4 times, 1 tr in each of next 25 (28:31:34) tr, 1 tr in 2nd ch. [105 (117:129:141) sts.]
Cont in tr, work one row.

### Divide for armholes and shape collar

**Row 1:** (RS) 1 dc in 1st tr, 2 ch, 1 tr in same tr, 1 tr in each of next 25 (28:31:34) tr, fasten off and break yarn, miss 4 tr, join yarn in next tr,

3 ch, 1 tr in each of next 44 (50:56:62) tr, fasten off and break yarn, miss 4 tr, join yarn in next tr, 3 ch, 1 tr in each of next 24 (27:30:33) tr, 2 tr in 2nd ch. [27 (30:33:36) sts in each front and 45 (51:57:63) sts in back.]

**Row 2:** 1 dc in 1st tr, 2 ch, 1 tr in same tr, 1 tr in each of next 23 (26:29:32) tr, 2trtog, 1 tr in 3rd ch, fasten off and break yarn, join yarn in 1st tr of back, 3 ch, 2trtog, 1 tr in each of next 39 (45:51:57) tr, 2trtog, 1 tr in 3rd ch, fasten off and break yarn, join yarn in 1st tr of right front, 3 ch, 2trtog, 1 tr in each of next 23 (26:29:32) tr, 2 tr in 2nd ch. [27 (30:33:36) sts in each front and 43 (49:55:61) sts in back.] Do not fasten off, leave back and fronts with yarn attached.

### SLEEVES (MAKE 2)

Make 15 (16:17:18) picots as given for back. Work Row 1 as given for back and fronts. [29 (31:33:35) sts.] Cont in tr as given for back, work 6 (6:2:2) rows.

**Inc row:** 1 dc in 1st tr, 2 ch, 1 tr in same tr, 1 tr in each tr to last st, 2 tr in 2nd ch. [31 (33:35:37) sts.]
Cont in tr, inc in this way at each end of 5 (5:6:6) foll 4th rows. [41 (43:47:49) sts.]
Work 1 row.

### Shape top

**Row 1:** (RS) Ss in each of first 4 tr, 3 ch, 1 tr in each of next 34 (36:40:42) tr, turn and leave

3 sts. [35 (37:41:43) sts.]

**Dec row:** 1 dc in 1st tr, 2 ch, 2trtog, 1 tr in each of next 29 (31:35:37) tr, 2trtog, 1 tr in 3rd ch. [33 (35:39:41) sts.] Fasten off.

## YOKE

**Row 1:** (RS) Across 27 (30:33:36) sts of right front work 1 dc in 1st tr, 2 ch, 1 tr in same tr, 1 tr in each of next 22 (25:28:31) tr, [2trtog] twice, across 33 (35:39:41) sts of right sleeve work * [2trtog] twice, 1 tr in each of next 25 (27:31:33) tr, [2trtog] twice *, across 43 (49:55:61) sts of back work [2trtog] twice, 1 tr in each of next 35 (41:47:53) tr, [2trtog] twice, rep from * to * across 33 (35:39:41) sts of left sleeve, across 27 (30:33:36) sts of left front work [2trtog] twice, 1 tr in each of next 22 (25:28:31) tr, 2 tr in 2nd ch. [149 (165:185:201) sts.]

**Row 2:** 1 dc in 1st tr, 2 ch, 1 tr in same tr, 1 tr in each of next 21 (24:27:30) tr, [2trtog] 4 times, 1 tr in each of next 21 (23:27:29) tr, [2trtog] 4 times, 1 tr in each of next 31 (37:43:49) tr, [2trtog] 4 times, 1 tr in each of next 21 (23:27:29) tr, [2trtog] 4 times, 1 tr in each of next 21 (24:27:30) tr, 2 tr in 2nd ch. [135 (151:171:187) sts.]

**Row 3:** 1 dc in 1st tr, 2 ch, 1 tr in same tr, 1 tr in each of next 20 (23:26:29) tr, [2trtog] 4 times, 1 tr in each of next 17 (19:23:25) tr, [2trtog] 4 times, 1 tr in each of next 27 (33:39:45) tr, [2trtog] 4 times, 1 tr in each

of next 17 (19:23:25) tr, [2trtog] 4 times, 1 tr in each of next 20 (23:26:29) tr, 2 tr in 2nd ch. [121 (137:157:173) sts.]

**Row 4:** 1 dc in 1st tr, 2 ch, 1 tr in same tr, 1 tr in each of next 19 (22:25:28) tr, [2trtog] 4 times, 1 tr in each of next 13 (15:19:21) tr, [2trtog] 4 times, 1 tr in each of next 23 (29:35:41) tr, [2trtog] 4 times, 1 tr in each of next 13 (15:19:21) tr, [2trtog] 4 times, 1 tr in each of next 19 (22:25:28) tr, 2 tr in 2nd ch. [107 (123:143:159) sts.]

**Row 5:** 1 dc in 1st tr, 2 ch, 1 tr in same tr, 1 tr in each of next 18 (21:24:27) tr, [2trtog] 4 times, 1 tr in each of next 9 (11:15:17) tr, [2trtog] 4 times, 1 tr in each of next 19 (25:31:37) tr, [2trtog] 4 times, 1 tr in each of next 9 (11:15:17) tr, [2trtog] 4 times, 1 tr in each of next 18 (21:24:27) tr, 2 tr in 2nd ch. [93 (109:129:145) sts.]

**Row 6:** 1 dc in 1st tr, 2 ch, 1 tr in same tr, 1 tr in each of next 17 (20:23:26) tr, [2trtog] 4 times, 1 tr in each of next 5 (7:11:13) tr, [2trtog] 4 times, 1 tr in each of next 15 (21:27:33) tr, [2trtog] 4 times, 1 tr in each of next 5 (7:11:13) tr, [2trtog] 4 times, 1 tr in each of next 17 (20:23:26) tr, 2 tr in 2nd ch. [79 (95:115:131) sts.]

*2nd size only*

**Row 7:** 1 dc in 1st tr, 2 ch, 1 tr in same tr, 1 tr in each of next 19 tr, [2trtog] 3 times, 1 tr in each of next 7 tr, [2trtog] 3 times, 1 tr in each of next 17 tr, [2trtog] 3 times, 1 tr in each of

next 7 tr, [2trtog] 3 times, 1 tr in each of next 19 tr, 2 tr in 2nd ch. [85 sts.]

### 3rd size only

**Row 7:** 1 dc in 1st tr, 2 ch, 1 tr in same tr, 1 tr in each of next 22 tr, [2trtog] 4 times, 1 tr in each of next 7 tr, [2trtog] 4 times, 1 tr in each of next 22 tr, [2trtog] 4 times, 1 tr in each of next 7 tr, [2trtog] 4 times, 1 tr in each of next 22 tr, 2 tr in 2nd ch. [101 sts.]

**Row 8:** 1 dc in 1st tr, 2 ch, 1 tr in same tr, 1 tr in each of next 21 tr, [2trtog] 3 times, 1 tr in each of next 7 tr, [2trtog] 3 times, 1 tr in each of next 19 tr, [2trtog] 3 times, 1 tr in each of

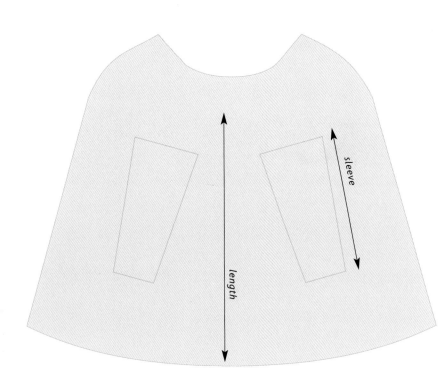

next 7 tr, [2trtog] 3 times, 1 tr in each of next 21 tr, 2 tr in 2nd ch. [91 sts.]

### 4th size only

**Row 7:** 1 dc in 1st tr, 2 ch, 1 tr in same tr, 1 tr in each of next 25 tr, [2trtog] 4 times, 1 tr in each of next 9 tr, [2trtog] 4 times, 1 tr in each of next 29 tr, [2trtog] 4 times, 1 tr in each of next 9 tr, [2trtog] 4 times, 1 tr in each of next 25 tr, 2 tr in 2nd ch. [117 sts.]

**Row 8:** 1 dc in 1st tr, 2 ch, 1tr in same tr, 1 tr in each of next 24 tr, [2trtog] 3 times, 1 tr in each of next 9 tr, [2trtog] 3 times, 1 tr in each of next 25 tr, [2trtog] 3 times, 1 tr in each of next 9 tr, [2trtog] 3 times, 1 tr in each of next 24 tr, 2tr in 2nd ch. [107 sts.]

**Row 9:** 1 dc in 1st tr, 2 ch, 1 tr in same tr, 1 tr in each of next 23 tr, [2trtog] 3 times, 1 tr in each of next 7 tr, [2trtog] 3 times, 1 tr in each of next 21 tr, [2trtog] 3 times, 1 tr in each of next 7 tr, [2trtog] 3 times, 1 tr in each of next 23 tr, 2tr in 2nd ch. [97 sts.]

### All sizes

[79 (85:91:97) sts.] Incs at front edges for collar have been completed.

**Next row:** 1 dc in 1st tr, 2 ch, 1 tr in each of next 18 (20:22:24) tr, [2trtog] twice, 1 tr in each of next 5 tr, [2trtog] twice, 1 tr in each of next 15 (17:19:21) tr, [2trtog] twice, 1 tr in each of next 5 tr, [2trtog] twice, 1 tr in each of next 18 (20:22:24) tr, 1 tr in 2nd ch. [71 (77:83:89) sts.]

**Next row:** 1 dc in 1st tr, 2 ch, 1 tr in each of

next 17 (19:21:23) tr, [2trtog] twice, 1 tr in each of next 3 tr, [2trtog] twice, 1 tr in each of next 13 (15:17:19) tr, [2trtog] twice, 1 tr in each of next 3 tr, [2trtog] twice, 1 tr in each of next 17 (19:21:23) tr, 1 tr in 2nd ch. [63 (69:75:81) sts.]

**Next row:** 1 dc in 1st tr, 2 ch, 1 tr in each of next 16 (18:20:22) tr, [2trtog] twice, 1 tr in next tr, [2trtog] twice, 1 tr in each of next 11 (13:15:17) tr, [2trtog] twice, 1 tr in next tr, [2trtog] twice, 1 tr in each of next 16 (18:20:22) tr, 1 tr in 2nd ch. [55 (61:67:73) sts.]
Cont in tr, work 11 rows. Fasten off.

## EDGING

With WS facing, join yarn at lower edge of left front. Spacing picots evenly, work up left front edge, along collar edge and down right front edge.
**Picot row:** 1 dc, 3 ch, ss in side of last dc, [2dc, 3ch, ss in side of last dc] to end.

## TIE BELT (OPTIONAL)

Make 65 (66:67:68) picots and work Row 1 as given for back and fronts. Work picot row as given for edging into Row 1. Fasten off.

## TO MAKE UP

Taking one st from each edge into seam, join sleeve seams. Join underarm seams. Try on coat and mark position for belt loops. Make a loop of crochet chain for each belt loop.

This flamboyant wrap will add a bright touch to any outfit. The pretty trefoil pattern is worked mostly in chain with the simple flowers and tassels added afterwards.

# TASSEL-EDGED WRAP

VERY EASY

## HELPFUL HINT

- The flower motifs are easy to do once you're confident about working different height stitches. Here's a reminder of how many times to take the yarn around the hook at beginning: dc = no times, hrt = once but pull through all loops first time; tr = once; dtr = twice, trtr = 3 times.

## MEASUREMENTS

**Actual width**
38 cm
15 in
**Actual length**
190 cm
75 in

## MATERIALS

- 7 × 50 g balls of Debbie Bliss Merino DK in yellow 503
- 4.00 mm crochet hook

## TENSION

One repeat measures 6.5 cm (2½ in). 10 rows to 10 cm (4 in) measured over trefoil chain pattern, each flower motif measures 7.5 cm (3 in) across, both when pressed, using 4.00 mm hook. Change hook size if necessary to obtain this tension.

## ABBREVIATIONS

*See page 9.*

## WRAP

**Row 1:** (WS) 16 ch, ss in 8th ch from hook, [7ch, ss in same ch as last ss] twice, * 23 ch, ss in 8th ch from hook, [7 ch, ss in same ch as last ss] twice, rep from * until there are 23 trefoil chain motifs, 8 ch, turn.
**Row 2:** Make 7 more ch, ss in 8th ch from hook, 7 ch, ss in same ch as last ss, 7 ch, 1 dc in 2nd 7 ch loop of next trefoil, * 7 ch, miss 7 ch on Row 1, ss in next ch, [7 ch, ss in same ch as last ss] 3 times, 7 ch, 1 dc in 2nd 7 ch loop of next trefoil, rep from * to last 8 ch, 7 ch, ss in last ch of 1st row, 7 ch, ss in same ch as last ss, 4 ch, 1 dtr in same ch as last ss, turn.
**Row 3:** 1 ch, 1 dc in dtr, * 7 ch, ss in next dc, [7 ch, ss in same dc as last ss] 3 times, 7 ch, 1 dc in 2nd 7 ch loop, rep from * to end, turn.
**Row 4:** [7 ch, ss in 1st dc] twice, 7 ch, 1 dc in 2nd 7 ch loop, * 7 ch, ss in next dc, [7 ch, ss in same dc as last ss] 3 times, 7 ch, 1 dc in 2nd 7 ch loop, rep from * to last dc, [7 ch, ss in last dc] twice, 4 ch, 1 dtr in last dc, turn.
Rows 3 and 4 form the pattern.
Work 17 more rows, so ending with a 3rd patt row. Fasten off.

*The starting chain for the trefoil chain pattern forms the first row and part of the second row.*

*Picking out the repeat to check your tension over the trefoil chain pattern can be difficult, so start by working a flower motif. If it is the right size, you've got the first one done (except for pulling back the last half petal to join) and your tension over the trefoil chain should be correct too.*

## FLOWER MOTIF

To form ring, wind yarn around first finger of left hand, insert hook, yrh and pull through. Work over end as well as into ring, then before joining on 1st round, pull end to tighten. Darn in end securely before trimming it off.

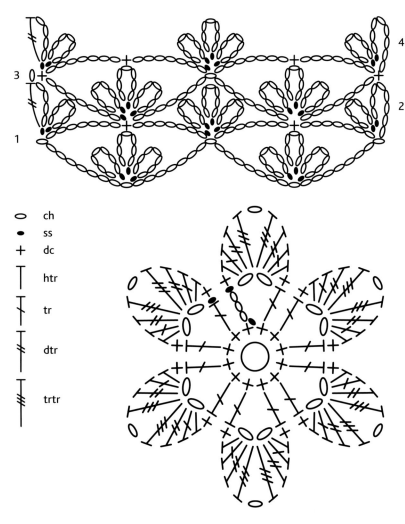

| | |
|---|---|
| ○ | ch |
| • | ss |
| + | dc |
| T | htr |
| T | tr |
| T | dtr |
| T | trtr |

### First motif

**Round 1:** (RS) 2 ch, work 12 dc in ring, ss in 1st dc.

**Round 2:** 3 ch, 1 tr in next dc, [2 ch, 1 tr in each of next 2 dc] 5 times, 2 ch, ss in 3rd ch.

**Round 3:** Ss in 1st tr, * [1 dc, 1 htr, 1 tr, 1 dtr, 1 trtr, 1 ch, 1 trtr, 1 dtr, 1 tr, 1 htr, 1 dc] all in next 2 ch space, rep from * 4 more times, in last 2 ch space, work 1 dc, 1 htr, 1 tr, 1 dtr, 1 trtr, with WS of wrap and flower motif together work 1 dc in centre 7 ch loop of first trefoil motif along lower edge of wrap, 1 trtr, 1 dtr, 1 tr, 1 htr, 1 dc in last 2 ch space, ss in 1st dc. Fasten off.

### 2nd and following motifs

Work as given for 1st motif until 4 petals of Round 3 have been completed. Join 5th petal with 1 dc in 1 ch space at centre of 1st petal of previous flower motif and 6th petal to next trefoil motif of wrap.

Continue until all trefoil motifs have a flower motif attached.

Make 3 more flowers, joining first one at corner and to adjacent flower, then second to edge and first flower, work third flower until 3 petals have been completed, join 4th petal to corner of wrap, 5th petal to edge and 6th petal to 2nd flower. Work 3 flowers for the other short edge in the same way.

Use nine 24-cm (9½ in) lengths of yarn folded in half plus a longer length to knot, wrap top to make a tassel for each flower. Use long end to sew tassels to flowers. Press. Trim tassels.

# CASUAL

There are times when you need a little stay-at-home, slouchy chic. The garments in this section are all about enjoying the feel of the yarns as you work the projects and the touch of the fabric when you wear the garments you've created. Luxuriate in the thick velvety surface of the chenille cowl or feel the contrast between soft cotton and silky ribbon in the tank top. Go for the gentle texture of the nubbly yarn used for the simple sweater, cover up in a bell-shaped, wool poncho, or for a sophisticated take on the casual look, choose the cardigan with frilled edge in creamy soft cashmere mix yarn.

# CHENILLE COWL

*This mini poncho is just a simple tube collar that increases out around the shoulders and ends in a fringe. Wear it indoors over a little top or pop it over a coat or jacket for an extra layer outdoors.*

🖐 *Do not count the 1 ch at the start of each round as a stitch.*

🖐 *Work the starting chain loosely.*

🖐 *Handle the yarn gently, coaxing the loops through quite loosely as you form the stitches. If you pull hard, the core of the yarn will lock and the stitches will be uneven or the yarn could break.*

🖐 *To join in new yarn, simply twist the ends together close to the work so the core at the centre of the yarn meets and links. To darn in the ends, strip off the velvet pile, knot the ends close to the join and darn in the remaining threads.*

## HELPFUL HINTS

- Wow! is a fat, velvety chenille yarn. Knot the yarn end before you start to crochet to prevent shedding. Snip off the knots to darn in the ends.
- The cowl is worked in rounds so there is no sewing up – simply darn in the ends and it's ready to wear!

## MEASUREMENTS

One size

**Actual measurement around neck edge**
55 cm
21½ in

**Actual measurement around lower edge**
110 cm
43¼ in

**Actual length (without fringe)**
35 cm
13¾ in

## MATERIALS

- 1 × 100 g ball of Sirdar Wow! in each of Cream Soda 755 (A), Pale Chamois 759 (B) and Light Suede 757 (C)
- 9.00 mm crochet hook

## TENSION

6 sts and 6 rows to 10 cm (4 in) measured over double crochet worked in rounds using 9.00 mm hook. Change hook size if necessary to obtain this tension.

## ABBREVIATIONS

See page 9.

## COWL

Using A, make 33 ch, ss in 1st ch to form a ring.

**Round 1:** 1 ch, 1 dc in each ch to end, ss in 1st dc. [33 sts.]

**Round 2:** 1 ch, 1 dc in each dc to end, ss in 1st dc. This round forms dc.

Cont in dc, work 8 more rounds.

**Inc round 1:** 1 ch, 1 dc in 1st dc, [2 dc in next dc, 1 dc in each of 2 foll dc] 10 times, 2 dc in next dc, 1 dc in foll dc, ss in 1st dc. [44 sts.]

Change to B. Work 3 rounds dc.

**Inc round 2:** 1 ch, 1 dc in 1st dc, [2 dc in next dc, 1 dc in foll dc] 21 times, 2 dc in last dc, ss in 1st dc. [66 sts.]

Cont in dc, work 3 more rounds.

Change to C. Work 3 rounds dc.

**Fringe round:** Using your fingers, pull a 10-cm (4-in) loop through first dc, from back to front of work and take yarn around base of loop close to edge, finish each dc around edge with a loop. Cut yarn. Darn in end securely.

## TO MAKE UP

Gently pull on each fringe loop to even out the twists. Darn in remaining ends. Roll collar down.

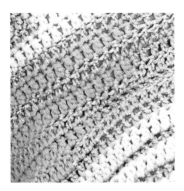

*This vest is very simple, there's just one band of contrast colour across the middle but random changes of matt and shiny textures in the ribbon yarn create a complex patchwork of contrast shapes without having to follow a chart or darn in lots of ends.*

# SHIMMERY TANK TOP

*This is one of the simplest garments to make, with no sleeve seams to match up and worked in simple stitches.*

## HELPFUL HINTS

- Ribbon yarn can unravel if the end is pulled. To prevent this, tie a knot in the end before starting to crochet. Snip off the knots before darning in the ends.
- The patterned effect will be different for each vest because of the random nature of the changes in colour

## MEASUREMENTS

### To fit bust

| 81 | 86 | 91 | 97 | 102 | 107 | cm |
|----|----|----|----|-----|-----|----|
| 32 | 34 | 36 | 38 | 40 | 42 | in |

### Actual width

| 82.5 | 88 | 93 | 98.5 | 104 | 109 | cm |
|------|----|----|------|-----|-----|----|
| 32½ | 34½ | 36½ | 38¾ | 41 | 43 | in |

### Actual length

| 46.5 | 47.5 | 48.5 | 52 | 53 | 54 | cm |
|------|------|------|----|----|----|----|
| 18¼ | 18¾ | 19 | 20½ | 21 | 21¼ | in |

*In the instructions figures are given for the smallest size first; larger sizes follow in brackets. Where only one set of figures is given this applies to all sizes.*

## MATERIALS

- 4 (4:5:5:6:6) × 50 g balls of Sirdar Duet in Ivory 744 (A)
- 1 (1:1:2:2:2) × 50 g balls of Sirdar Duet in Chamois 741 (B)
- 4.50 mm crochet hook

## TENSION

15 sts and 9 rows to 10 cm (4 in) measured over treble patt using 4.50 mm hook. Change hook size if necessary to obtain this tension.

## ABBREVIATIONS

**3trtog** – leaving last loop of each st on hook, work a treble in each of next 3 sts, yrh and pull through 4 loops on hook
*See also page 9.*

# TOP

## BACK

Using A, make 64 (68:72:76:80:84) ch.
**Row 1:** (WS) Work 1 tr in 4th ch from hook, 1 tr in each ch to end.
[62 (66:70:74:78:82) sts.]
**Row 2:** 1 dc in 1st tr, 2 ch, 1 tr in each tr to last st, 1 tr in 3rd ch.
This row forms tr patt.
Working into 2nd ch at end of foll rows, cont in tr, work 14 more rows.
Change to B. Work 7 (7:7:8:8:8) rows.
Change to A. Work 2 (2:2:3:3:3) rows.

### Shape armholes

**Next row:** (RS) Ss in each of first 3 tr, 1 dc in next tr, 2 ch, 1 tr in each tr to last 3 sts, turn.
[56 (60:64:68:72:76) sts.]

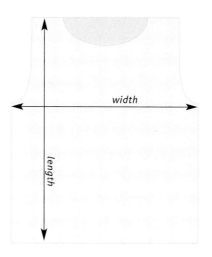

*width*

*length*

**Dec row:** 1 dc in 1st tr, 2 ch, 3trtog, 1 tr in each tr to last 4 sts, 3trtog, 1 tr in 2nd ch. [52 (56:60:64:68:72) sts.]
Cont in tr, dec two sts in this way at each end of next 1 (2:2:2:3:3) rows.
[48 (48:52:56:56:60) sts **.]
Cont in tr, work 14 (14:15:16:16:17) rows. Fasten off.

## FRONT

Work as given for back to **.
Cont in tr, work 4 (4:5:6:6:7) rows.

### Shape neck

**Next row:** 1 dc in 1st tr, 2 ch, 1 tr in each of next 17 (17:18:20:20:21) tr, turn and complete first side on these
18 (18:19:21:21:22) sts. Cont in tr, dec 2 sts by working 3trtog one st in from neck edge on next 4 rows. [10 (10:11:13:13:14) sts.]
Work 5 rows straight. Fasten off. Leave centre 12 (12:14:14:14:16) tr, join yarn in next tr, 3 ch, 1 tr in each tr to end.
[18 (18:19:21:21:22) sts.] Complete to match first side.

## TO MAKE UP

Matching sts, join shoulders.

### Neck edging

With RS facing, join A at right shoulder. Work 1 dc in first tr of back neck, 2 ch, 1 tr in each of 27 (27:29:29:29:31) tr across back neck, 19 tr in row-ends down left front neck, 1 tr in each of 12 (12:14:14:14:16) tr across front neck and 19 tr in row-ends up right front neck, ss in 2nd ch. Fasten off.

### Armhole edgings

With RS facing, join A to first tr at underarm. Work 1 dc in first tr, 2 ch, 1 tr in each of next 2 tr, 34 (36:38:40:42:44) tr in row-ends to shoulder, 1 tr in seam, 34 (36:38:40:42:44) tr in row ends to underarm and 1 tr in each of next 3 sts. Fasten off.
Join side and armhole edging seams.

*This skinny-fit sweater is worked all in simple treble crochet. The softly textured yarn creates a rich, textured effect and, because it is stretchy, creates a close-fitting garment.*

# SIMPLE TEXTURED SWEATER

*When shaping the sleeves, place markers at each end of every inc row to make it easier to keep track of the number of incs worked. The markers will also help match the row-ends when sewing up.*

*Sewing up with textured yarn is simple if you have the RS of the work facing, and use mattress stitch and a blunt-pointed needle.*

## HELPFUL HINTS

- The yarn alternates between thin, smooth threads and soft, furry nubs. Textured yarns can be difficult to work with but this one is easy because the hook catches the smooth parts of the yarn neatly and the thicker bits pull through easily.

## MEASUREMENTS

### To fit bust

| | | | | | |
|---|---|---|---|---|---|
| 81 | 86 | 91 | 97 | 102 | cm |
| 32 | 34 | 36 | 38 | 40 | in |

### Actual bust

| | | | | | |
|---|---|---|---|---|---|
| 81 | 87.5 | 93.5 | 100 | 106 | cm |
| 32 | 34½ | 36¾ | 39½ | 41¾ | in |

### Actual length

| | | | | | |
|---|---|---|---|---|---|
| 52 | 53 | 54 | 55 | 56 | cm |
| 20½ | 21 | 21¼ | 21½ | 22 | in |

### Actual sleeve

46 cm (18 in)

*In the instructions figures are given for the smallest size first; larger sizes follow in brackets. Where only one set of figures is given this applies to all sizes.*

## MATERIALS

- 8 (9:10:11:12) × 50 g balls of Sirdar Fresco in Faded Denim 804
- 4.00 mm crochet hook

## TENSION

16 sts and 10 rows to 10 cm (4 in) over treble using 4.00 mm hook. Change hook size if necessary to obtain this tension.

## ABBREVIATIONS

**2trtog** – leaving last loop of each st on hook, work a treble in each of next 2 sts, yrh and pull through 3 loops on hook.

**3trtog** – leaving last loop of each st on hook, work a treble in each of next 3 sts, yrh and pull through 4 loops on hook.

*See also page 9.*

# SWEATER

## BACK

Make 61 (66:71:76:81) ch.

**Row 1:** (WS) 1 tr in 4th ch from hook, 1 tr in each ch to end. [59 (64:69:74:79) sts.]

**Row 2:** 3 ch, miss 1st tr, 1 tr in each tr to last st, 1 tr in 3rd ch.

Row 2 forms treble crochet. Cont in tr, work 19 more rows.

**Inc row:** (RS) 3 ch, 1 tr in 1st tr usually missed, 1 tr in each tr to last st, 2 tr in 3rd ch. [61 (66:71:76:81) sts.] Cont in tr, inc in this way at each end of next 2 RS rows. [65 (70:75:80:85) sts.]

Cont in tr, work 7 rows.

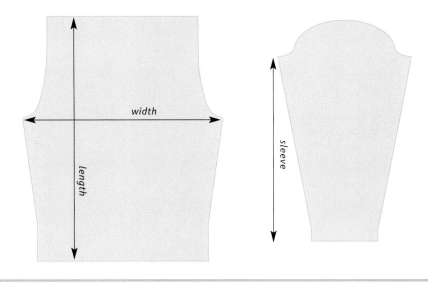

*width*

*length*

*sleeve*

**Shape armholes**

**Next row:** (RS) Ss in each of 1st 3 tr, 3 ch, miss tr with last ss, 1 tr in each tr to last 2 sts, turn. [61 (66:71:76:81) sts.]

**Dec row:** 3 ch, miss 1st tr, 2trtog, 1 tr in each tr to last 2 sts, 2trtog. [59 (64:69:74:79) sts.] Cont in tr dec in this way at each end of next 5 (6:6:7:7) rows. [49 (52:57:60:65) sts **.] Cont in tr, work 12 (12:13:13:14) rows. Fasten off.

### FRONT

Work as given for back to **. Cont in tr, work 8 (8:9:9:10) rows.

### Shape neck

**Next row:** 3 ch, miss 1st tr, 1 tr in each of next 13 (14:15:16:18) tr, turn and complete right side on these 14 (15:16:17:19) sts. Cont in tr, dec by working 2trtog at neck edge on next 3 rows. [11 (12:13:14:16) sts.] Fasten off. Leave centre 21 (22:25:26:27) tr, join yarn in next tr, 3 ch, miss tr joined into, 1 tr in each st to end. [14 (15:16:17:19) sts.] Cont in tr, dec by working 2trtog at neck edge on next 3 rows. [11 (12:13:14:16) sts.] Fasten off.

### SLEEVES (MAKE 2)

Make 28 (30:34:36:40) ch.

**Row 1:** (WS) 1 tr in 4th ch from hook, 1 tr in each ch to end. [26 (28:32:34:38) sts.]

**Row 2:** 3 ch, miss 1st tr, 1 tr in each tr to last st, 1 tr in 3rd ch.

Row 2 forms treble crochet. Cont in tr, work 3 more rows. Inc in same way as back at each end of next row and on 13 foll 3rd rows. [54 (56:60:62:66) sts.] Work 1 row.

### Shape top

**Next row:** Ss in each of 1st 3 tr, 3 ch, miss tr with last ss, 1 tr in each tr to last 2 sts, turn. [50 (52:56:58:62) sts.] Cont in tr, dec in same way as back at each end of next 6 (7:7:8:8) rows. [38 (38:42:42:46) sts.]

**Next row:** 3 ch, miss 1st tr, 3trtog, 1 tr in each tr to last 3 sts, 3trtog. [34 (34:38:38:42) sts.] Work last row 1 (1:2:2:3) more times. [30 sts.] Fasten off.

### NECKBAND

Matching sts, join shoulders. With RS facing, join yarn in 1st tr of back neck, 3 ch, 1 tr in each of next 26 (27:30:31:32) tr across back neck, 10 tr in row-ends down left front neck, 1 tr in each of 21 (22:25:26:27) tr across front neck, 10 tr in row-ends up right front neck, ss in 3rd ch. [68 (70:76:78:80) sts.] Turn. 3 ch, miss 1st tr, 1 tr in each tr to end, ss in 3rd ch. Fasten off.

### TO MAKE UP

Set in sleeves. Join side and sleeve seams.

# VARIATION

## SPORTY HEADBAND

Make a fashionable, sporty headband using any leftover yarn, or the same yarn in a contrasting colour. Make 12 ch.

**Row 1:** (WS) 1 tr in 4th ch from hook, 1 tr in each ch to end. [10 sts.]

**Row 2:** 3 ch, miss 1st tr, 1 tr in each tr to last st, 1 tr in 3rd ch. 2nd row forms treble crochet. Cont in tr, working until band, when slightly stretched, fits around head. Fasten off. Join ends.

*This pretty poncho is made from eight-sided motifs joined in rounds to give a bell shape that curves out over the shoulders.*

# FLOWER MOTIF PONCHO

 ★★★ MEDIUM

*Instructions are given to work all the motifs, then join them. If you prefer, you could join the motifs and work the edging each time you complete enough motifs to make a round.*

*Always darn in the end from the starting ring, don't just snip it off.*

*Save time making up and darn in ends as you go.*

## HELPFUL HINTS

• If you are really short of time you can make a simpler, shorter version of the poncho, like a little shoulder cape. You'll only need to crochet 24 motifs, then finish the poncho after assembling the first and second rounds of motifs. You'll need just 5 balls of yarn.

## MEASUREMENTS

One size
**Actual length**
54 cm
21¼ in

## MATERIALS

• 10 × 50 g balls of Debbie Bliss Merino DK in Pink 615
• 3.50 mm crochet hook

## TENSION

Each motif measures 9.5 cm (3¾ in), when pressed, using 3.50 mm hook. Change hook size if necessary to obtain this size motif.

## ABBREVIATIONS

**3trtrcl** – leaving last loop of each st on hook, work 3trtr, yrh and pull through 4 loops on hook
*See also page 9.*

# PONCHO

## FLOWER OCTAGON MOTIF

Wind yarn around first finger to form a ring.
**Round 1:** (RS) 5 ch, leaving last loop of each st on hook, work 2 trtr in ring, yrh and pull through 3 loops on hook, [5 ch, 3trtrcl in ring] 7 times, 2 ch, 1 tr in 5th ch, pull end to tighten ring.
**Round 2:** 1 ch, 1 dc in first sp, 6 ch, [1 dc in next 5 ch sp, 6 ch] 7 times, ss in 1st dc.
**Round 3:** Ss in first 6 ch sp, 3 ch, 6 tr in first 6 ch sp, 3 ch [7 tr in next 6 ch cp, 3 ch] 7 times, ss in 3rd ch. Fasten off.

Make 56 flower octagon motifs.

### Join 1st line of 8 motifs

With RS together, join two motifs by working 1 dc into 3 ch sp, 1 dc into each of the 7 tr along one edge, 1 dc in 3 ch sp. Open out motifs and leaving one edge at top for neckline and 5 edges below free, continue to join 6 more motifs in the same way, then join 8th motif to 7th, then to 1st to form a ring.

### Join 2nd line of 16 motifs

Join 2 motifs in same way as 1st line of motifs. Open out motifs and leaving 3 edges at each side, continue to join 14 more motifs in the same way, then join 16th motif to 15th, then to 1st to form a ring.

### Join 3rd and 4th lines of motifs

Join 16 motifs in same way as 2nd line of motifs.

### Lower edge of 1st line of motifs

Join yarn in last free 3 ch sp of 8th joined motif at lower edge of 1st line of motifs.

**Round 1:** (RS) 1 ch, 3 dc in same 3 ch sp as joined yarn, ** 3 dc in 1st 3 ch sp of next motif, 3 ch, * miss 1 tr, [1 tr in next tr, 1 ch, miss 1 tr] 3 times, work [1 tr, 1 ch] twice in next 3 ch sp, rep from * once, miss 1 tr, [1 tr in next tr, 1 ch, miss 1 tr] 3 times, work 2 more ch, 3 dc in last 3 ch sp of this motif, rep from ** 7 times, omitting last 3 dc of last rep, ss in 1st dc.

**Round 2:** 4 ch, miss 4 dc, 1 dtr in next dc, 3 ch, * 1 dtr in 1st tr, [1 dtr in next sp, 1 dtr in next tr] 12 times **, yrh 4 times, insert hook in 1st dc of next 3 dc group, yrh and pull loop through [yrh and pull through 2 loops on hook] twice, yrh twice, insert hook in last dc of foll 3 dc group, yrh and pull loop through, [yrh and pull through 2 loops on hook] twice, yrh and pull through 3 loops on hook, [yrh and pull through 2 loops on hook] twice, rep from * 6 more times, then work from * to **, ss in 3rd ch. [208 sts.]

**Round 3:** 4 ch, miss 1 dtr, [1 tr in next st, 1 ch, miss one st] to end, ss in 3rd ch.

### Join edging and 2nd line of motifs

**Round 1:** 1 ch, 1 dc in same place as ss, 1 dc in next sp, 1 dc in next tr, with RS tog, join top edge of 1st motif of 2nd line of motifs with dc by working * 2 sps tog, [next tr from each edge tog, foll sp and tr tog] 3 times, then work next tr from each edge tog and foll 2 sps tog *, 1 dc in next tr, 1 dc in next sp, 1 dc in next tr, rep from * to * to join 2nd motif, [1 dc in next tr, 1 dc in next sp] twice, 1 dc in foll tr, cont joining motifs, working 5 dc and 3 dc alternately in edge between joining motifs until all 16 motifs have been joined ending 1 dc in last tr, 1 dc in last sp, ss in 1st dc. Fasten off.

### Lower edge of 2nd line of motifs

Join yarn to 2nd tr of 1st motif.

**Round 1:** 4 ch, * [miss one st, 1 tr in next tr or sp, 1 ch] 10 times, 1 tr in 2nd tr of next motif, 1 ch, rep from * to end, omitting last tr and ch, ss in 3rd ch. Fasten off.

Join yarn in 3rd sp of Round 1.

**Round 2:** 4 ch, * [1 dtr in next tr, 1 dtr in next sp] 5 times, yrh 4 times, miss one sp, insert hook in next sp, yrh and pull loop through, [yrh and pull through 2 loops on hook] twice, yrh twice, miss one sp, insert hook in foll sp, yrh and pull loop through [yrh and pull through 2 loops on hook] twice, yrh and pull through 3 loops on hook, [yrh and pull through 2 loops on hook] twice, miss one sp,

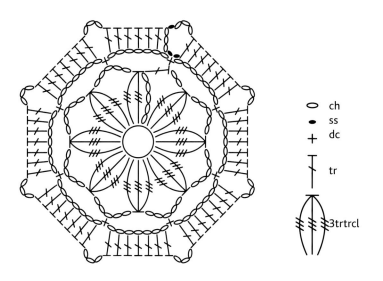

Key:
- ◯ ch
- ● ss
- + dc
- ⊤ tr
- 3trtrcl

1 dtr in next sp, rep from * to end, omitting last dtr, ss in 4th ch.

**Round 3:** 4 ch, [1 tr in next dtr, 1 ch] to end, ss in 3rd ch. Fasten off.

Join yarn in 5th sp from end of Round 3.

### Join edging and 3rd line of motifs

**Round 1:** 1 ch, with RS tog, join top edge of 1st motif of 3rd line of motifs with dc by working * 2 sps tog, [next tr and sp tog] 7 times, then work foll 2 sps tog, 2 dc in each of next 3 sps, rep from * to end, ss in 1st dc. Fasten off.

### Lower edge of 3rd line of motifs

Work 3 rounds as given for lower edge of 2nd line of motifs.

### Join edging and 4th line of motifs

Work as given for join edging and 3rd line of motifs.

### Lower edge of 4th line of motifs

Work 3 rounds as given for lower edge of 2nd line of motifs but turn instead of fastening off after Round 3.

**Round 4:** 1 ch, 2 dc in each sp to end, ss in 1st dc. Fasten off.

### COLLAR

With RS facing, join yarn to a 3 ch sp at beg of a motif at top edge of 1st line of motifs.

**Round 1:** (RS) 4 ch, miss 1st tr, [1 tr in next tr, 1 ch, miss next tr] 3 times, [1 tr in 3 ch sp, 1 ch] twice, rep from * 7 more times, omitting last tr and ch, ss in 3rd ch.

**Round 2:** 4 ch, 1 dtr in 1st 1 ch sp, [1 dtr in next tr, 1 dtr in next sp] to end, ss in 4th ch. [80 sts.]

**Round 3:** 4 ch, 1 dtr in each dtr to end, ss in 4th ch.

Cont in dtr, work 6 more rounds. Fasten off.

### TO MAKE UP

Darn in ends. Press according to ball band. Roll collar down.

*length*

*This soft, supple cashmere mix yarn is a joy to handle and gives an exquisite quality to the easy-to-work, double and treble stitch pattern used for this sophisticated but simple cardigan.*

# CARDIGAN WITH FRILLED EDGE

★★☆ EASY

*Work the starting chain quite loosely, if necessary, use one size larger hook.*

*Instead of the usual 3 ch, a dc and 2 ch is worked at the start of each treble row to close the gap between the first and second stitches. Stretch the loop on the hook slightly before making the dc.*

*The 1 ch at the start of a dc row does not count as a stitch.*

## HELPFUL HINTS
● Keep your work clean by storing it in a pillow case.

## MEASUREMENTS
### To fit bust

| 81 | 86 | 91 | 97 | 102 | 107 | 112 | cm |
|----|----|----|----|-----|-----|-----|-----|
| 32 | 34 | 36 | 38 | 40 | 42 | 44 | in |

### Actual bust

| 89 | 95 | 101 | 107 | 113 | 120 | 126 | cm |
|----|----|-----|-----|-----|-----|-----|-----|
| 35 | 37½ | 39¾ | 42 | 44½ | 47¼ | 49½ | in |

### Actual length

| 60.5 | 60.5 | 62.5 | 62.5 | 64.5 | 64.5 | 66 | cm |
|------|------|------|------|------|------|-----|-----|
| 24 | 24 | 24½ | 24½ | 25¼ | 25¼ | 26 | in |

### Actual sleeve
48 cm
19 in

*In the instructions figures are given for the smallest size first; larger sizes follow in brackets. Where only one set of figures is given this applies to all sizes.*

## MATERIALS
● 15 (16:16:17:18:18:19) × 50 g balls of Debbie Bliss Cashmerino Aran in 101
● 5.00 mm crochet hook

## TENSION
13 sts and 11 rows to 10 cm (4 in) measured over double crochet and treble pattern using 5.00 mm hook. Change hook size if necessary to obtain this tension.

## ABBREVIATIONS
**3trtog** – leaving last loop of each st on hook, work a treble in each of next 3 sts, yrh and pull through 4 loops on hook
*See also page 9.*

# CARDIGAN

## BACK
Make 51 (55:59:63:67:71:75) ch.
**Row 1:** (WS) 1 dc in 2nd ch from hook, 1 dc in each ch to end. [50 (54:58:62:66:70:74) sts.]
**Row 2:** 1 dc in 1st dc, 2 ch, 1 tr in each dc to end.
**Row 3:** 1 ch, 1 dc in each tr to last st, 1dc in 2nd ch.
Rows 2 and 3 form dc and tr patt. Cont in patt, work 20 more rows, ending with a 3rd patt row.
**Inc row:** (RS) 1 dc in 1st dc, 2 ch, 1 tr in 1st dc, 1 tr in each dc to last dc, 2 tr in last dc. [52 (56:60:64:68:72:76) sts.]
Cont in patt, inc in this way at each end of 3 foll 6th rows. [58 (62:66:70:74:78:82) sts.]
Cont in patt, work 3 rows, ending with a 3rd patt row.

## Shape armholes

**Next row:** (RS) Ss in each of first 3 (3:4:4:5:5:6) dc, 3 ch, miss dc with ss, 1 tr in each dc to last 2 (2:3:3:4:4:5) dc, turn. [54 (58:60:64:66:70:72) sts.] Patt 1 row.

**Dec row:** 1 dc in first dc, 2 ch, 3trtog, 1 tr in each dc to last 4 sts, 3trtog, 1 tr in last dc. [50 (54:56:60:62:66:68) sts.]

Patt 1 row. Work dec row again. [46 (50:52:56:58:62:64) sts.]

Patt 1 row. Work dec row again. [42 (46:48:52:54:58:60) sts.]

Patt 15 (15:17:17:19:19:21) rows, ending with a 3rd patt row. Fasten off.

## LEFT FRONT

Make 33 (35:37:39:41:43:45) ch.

**Row 1:** (WS) 1 dc in 2nd ch from hook, 1 dc in each ch to end. [32 (34:36:38:40:42:44) sts.]

**Row 2:** 1 dc in 1st dc, 2 ch, 1 tr in each dc to end.

**Row 3:** 1 ch, 1 dc in each tr to last st, 1 dc in 2nd ch.

Rows 2 and 3 form dc and tr patt. Cont in patt, work 20 more rows, ending with a 3rd patt row **.

**Inc row:** (RS) 1 dc in 1st dc, 2 ch, 1 tr in 1st dc, 1 tr in each dc to end. [33 (35:37:39:41:43:45) sts.]

Cont in patt, inc in this way at beg of 3 foll 6th rows. [36 (38:40:42:44:46:48) sts.] Cont in patt, work 3 rows, ending with a 3rd patt row.

## Shape armhole

**Next row:** (RS) Ss in each of first 3
(3:4:4:5:5:6) dc, 3 ch, miss dc with ss, 1 tr in
each dc to end. [34 (36:37:39:40:42:43) sts.]
Patt 1 row.
**Dec row:** 1 dc in first dc, 2 ch, 3trtog, 1 tr in
each dc to end. [32 (34:35:37:38:40:41) sts.]
Patt 1 row. Work dec row again.
[30 (32:33:35:36:38:39) sts.]
Patt 1 row. Work dec row again.
[28 (30:31:33:34:36:37) sts.]
Patt 9 (9:11:11:13:13:15) rows, ending with a
3rd patt row.

## Shape neck

**Row 1:** (RS) 1 dc in 1st dc, 2 ch, 1 tr in each
of next 8 (10:11:12:13:14:15) dc, 3trtog,
1 tr in next dc, turn and leave
15 (15:15:16:16:17:17) dc for neck.
[11 (13:14:15:16:17:18) sts.] Patt 1 row.
**Row 3:** 1 dc in 1st dc, 2 ch, 1 tr in each dc to
last 4 dc, 3trtog, 1 tr in last dc. [9 (11:12:13:
14:15:16) sts.] Patt 3 rows. Fasten off.

## RIGHT FRONT

Work as given for Left Front to **.
**Inc row:** (RS) 1 dc in 1st dc, 2 ch, 1 tr in each
dc to last dc, 2 tr in last dc.
[33 (35:37:39:41:43:45) sts.] Cont in patt, inc
in this way at end of 3 foll 6th rows.
[36 (38:40:42:44:46:48) sts.] Cont in patt,
work 3 rows, ending with a 3rd patt row.

## Shape armhole

**Next row:** (RS) 1 dc in 1st dc, 2 ch, 1 tr in
each dc to last 2 (2:3:3:4:4:5) dc, turn.
[34 (36:37:39:40:42:43) sts.] Patt 1 row.
**Dec row:** (RS) 1 dc in first dc, 2 ch, 1 tr in
each dc to last 4 sts, 3trtog, 1 tr in last dc.
[32 (34:35:37:38:40:41) sts.]
Patt 1 row. Work dec row again.
[30 (32:33:35:36:38:39) sts.]
Patt 1 row. Work dec row again.
[28 (30:31:33:34:36:37) sts.]
Patt 9 (9:11:11:13:13:15) rows, ending with a
3rd patt row. Fasten off. With RS facing, leave
first 15 (15:15:16:16:17:17) dc for neck.

## Shape neck

**Row 1:** (RS) Join yarn and work 1 dc in next
dc, 2 ch, 3trtog, 1 tr in each dc to end.
[11 (13:14:15:16:17:18) sts.] Patt 1 row.
**Row 3:** 1 dc in 1st dc, 2 ch, 3trtog, 1 tr in
each dc to end. [9 (11:12:13:14:15:16) sts.]
Patt 3 rows. Fasten off.

## SLEEVES (MAKE 2)

Make 31 (31:31:35:35:39:39) ch.
**Row 1:** (WS) 1 dc in 2nd ch from hook, 1 dc
in each ch to end.
[30 (30:30:34:34:38:38) sts.] Work in dc and
tr patt as given for back for 4 rows.
Cont in patt, inc in same way as back at each
end of next row and on 6 (7:7:7:7:7:7) foll 6th
rows. [44 (46:46:50:50:54:54) sts.]

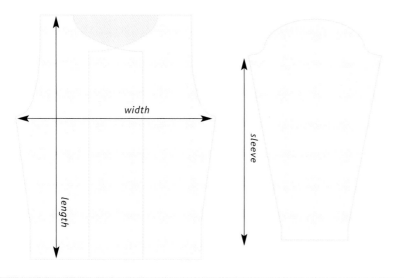

width

sleeve

length

## VARIATION

If you'd like just a small shell edging, finish the fronts and neck edge with Row 1 and Row 6 of front and neck edging as given for the cuffs. If you do this, you'll need one less ball of yarn.

Inc at each end of next 0 (0:1:0:1:0:2) RS rows. [44 (46:48:50:52:54:58) sts.] Patt 11 (5:3:5:3:5:1) rows.

### Shape top

**Next row:** (RS) Ss in each of first 3 (3:4:4:5:5:6) dc, 3 ch, miss dc with ss, 1 tr in each dc to last 2 (2:3:3:4:4:5) dc, turn. [40 (42:42:44:44:46:48) sts.] Patt 1 row.

**Dec row:** 1 dc in first dc, 2 ch, 3trtog, 1 tr in each dc to last 4 sts, 3trtog, 1 tr in last dc. [36 (38:38:40:40:42:44) sts.]
Dec in this way at each end of next 6 RS rows. [12 (14:14:16:16:18:20) sts.]
Patt 1 (1:3:1:3:1:3) rows. Fasten off.

### EDGINGS

#### Preparation for front and neck edging

Matching sts, join shoulders. With WS facing, work 87 (87:91:91:95:95:99) dc up left front edge to start of neck shaping. Fasten off. Starting at neck edge, work 86 (86:90:90:94:94:98) dc along right front edge. Fasten off. With WS of left front facing, join yarn after 15 (15:15:16:16:17:17) dc at neck and work 9 dc around shaped edge to shoulder. Fasten off. Starting at shoulder, work right front neck to match.

### Front and neck edging

**Row 1:** (RS) Join yarn with a dc in 1st dc of right front edge, * [miss 1 dc, 4 tr in next dc, miss 1 dc, 1 dc in next dc] * 21 (21:22:22:23:23:24) times up right front edge, miss 1 dc, 4 tr in corner dc, miss 1 dc, 1 dc in next dc, rep from * to * 17 (17:17:18:18:19:19) times around neck edge, miss 1 dc, 4 tr in corner dc, miss 1 dc, 1 dc in next dc, rep from * to * 21 (21:22:22:23:23:24) times down left front edge.

**Rows 2 and 4:** 1 ch, 1 dc in each st to end.

**Row 3:** 1 dc in 1st dc, 2 ch, 1 tr in same dc, [2 tr in each dc] to end.

**Row 5:** 1 dc in 1st dc, 2 ch, [1 tr in each dc] to end, do not turn.

**Row 6:** (RS) Working from left to right, work 1 dc in each st. Fasten off.

### TO MAKE UP

Press according to ball band. Set in sleeves. Taking one st in from each edge, join side and sleeve seams.

#### Cuff edging

With RS facing join yarn with a dc in sleeve seam and work around edge as given for Row 1 of front and neck edging, then work Row 6 of front and neck edging. Fasten off.

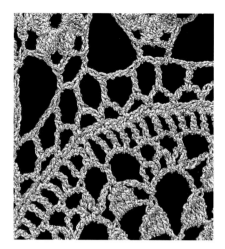

# GLAMOROUS

When it's party time, crochet comes into the spotlight. Whether your personal style is full-on glitz or you just want to spark up a plain outfit you'll find something special here. Create an unforgettable image with the stunning, vintage-look circular waistcoat or revel in the sexy shine of a sequin-trimmed vest. Layer the long pointed-edge waistcoat over trousers or a dress. Keep your shoulders cosy with a fabulous frilled wrap in fine mohair, the shell-edged shrug in angora-mix yarn or the faux fur blue capelet. And for a touch of shine day or night, add the skinny, beaded gold scarf to any outfit.

# GOLD CIRCLE WAISTCOAT

*This unusual waistcoat is made from a huge circle of lacy crochet. In fine metallic yarn, it has a fantastic vintage feel.*

🖐 *The back and fronts of the waistcoat are worked in one big circle, starting from the centre back and working in rounds. Spaces are left for the armholes, then the circle is continued to form the fronts and collar.*

🖐 *When working 3 or more chain to stand for a stitch at the start of a round, make the last chain slightly loosely so it's easier to work the slip stitch under both strands of the loop when joining the round.*

🖐 *Darn in the end from the starting ring very thoroughly.*

## HELPFUL HINTS

- This garment is very flexible, because it's not made in the usual way, it stretches and drapes to give a flattering fit.
- You can fasten your waistcoat with just one button under the bust as shown or you could pin the fronts together with a brooch, use a ribbon tie or lace them together.
- If you'd like to do up the front more, simply sew on more buttons.
- Mark the buttonhole fan, maybe with a tiny loop of yarn on the wrong side, so you can find it easily.

## MEASUREMENTS

### To fit bust

| | | | |
|---|---|---|---|
| 81–86 | 91–97 | 102–107 | cm |
| 32–34 | 36–38 | 40–42 | in |

### Actual width (across circle at widest)

| | | | |
|---|---|---|---|
| 86 | 96 | 106 | cm |
| 34 | 37¾ | 41¾ | in |

### Actual length (at centre back with 14 cm (5½ in) folded down for collar)

| | | | |
|---|---|---|---|
| 72 | 82 | 92 | cm |
| 28¼ | 32¼ | 36¼ | in |

*In the instructions figures are given for the smallest size first; larger sizes follow in brackets. Where only one set of figures is given this applies to all sizes.*

## MATERIALS

- 10 (12:14) × 25 g balls of Rowan Lurex Shimmer in Antique White Gold 332
- 2.50 mm crochet hook
- 1 button

## TENSION

The first 5 rounds of centre back circle measure 11 cm (4¼ in), 14 rounds measure 31 cm (12 in) across using 2.50 mm hook. Change hook size if necessary to obtain this size circle.

## ABBREVIATIONS

**5dtrcl** – leaving least loop of each st on hook, work 5dtr, yrh and pull through all 6 loops on hook
*See also page 9.*

# WAISTCOAT

## BACK

Wind yarn around finger to form a ring.
**Round 1:** (RS) 3 ch, 23 tr in ring, pull end to close ring, ss in 3rd ch. [24 sts.]
**Round 2:** 4 ch, miss 1st st, [1 tr in next tr, 1 ch] 23 times, ss in 3rd ch.
**Round 3:** 5 ch, miss 1st st, [1 tr in next tr, 2 ch] 23 times, ss in 3rd ch.
**Round 4:** 6 ch, miss 1st st, [1 tr in next tr, 3 ch] 23 times, ss in 3rd ch.
**Round 5:** 7 ch, miss 1st st, [1 tr in next tr, 4 ch] 23 times, ss in 3rd ch.

**Round 6:** 8 ch, miss 1st st, [1 tr in next tr, 5 ch] 23 times, ss in 3rd ch.

**Round 7:** 4 ch, leaving last loop of each st on hook, work 4 dtr in first 5 ch sp, yrh and pull through all 5 loops on hook, [5 ch, 1 dc in next 5 ch sp, 5 ch, 5dtrcl in foll 5 ch sp] 11 times, 5 ch, 1 dc in next 5 ch sp, 2 ch, 1 tr in 4th ch.

**Round 8:** 4 ch, leaving last loop of each st on hook, work 4 dtr in sp formed by tr, yrh and pull through 5 loops on hook, 5 ch, 5dtrcl in next 5 ch sp, [10 ch, 5dtrcl in next 5 ch sp, 5 ch, 5dtrcl in foll 5 ch sp] 11 times, 10 ch, ss in 4th ch.

**Round 9:** Ss in 1st 5 ch sp, 4 ch, leaving last loop of each st on hook, work 4 dtr in first 5 ch sp, yrh and pull through 5 loops on hook, * 5 ch, 1 dc in next 10 ch sp, [5 ch, 1 dc in same 10 ch sp] 3 times, 5 ch, 5dtrcl in next 5 ch sp, rep from * 10 more times, 5 ch, 1 dc in next 10 ch sp, [5 ch, 1 dc in same 10 ch sp] 3 times, 5 ch, ss in 4th ch.

**Round 10:** 8 ch, * 1 tr in next 3 ch sp, [3 ch, 1 tr in foll 3 ch sp] twice, 5 ch, 1 tr in 5dtrcl, 5 ch, rep from * 10 more times, 1 tr in next 3 ch sp, [3 ch, 1 tr in foll 3 ch sp] twice, 5 ch, ss in 3rd ch.

**Round 11:** Ss in 1st sp, 5 ch, [1 dtr, 1 ch] twice in same sp, * [1 dtr, 1 ch] twice in each of next two 3 ch sps, [1 dtr, 1 ch] 3 times in each of next two 5 ch sps, rep from * 10 times, [1 dtr, 1 ch] twice in each of next

two 3 ch sps, [1 dtr, 1 ch] 3 times in next 5 ch sp, ss in 4th ch.

**Round 12:** 1 ch, 2 dc in each 1 ch sp to end, ss in 1st dc. [240 sts.]

**Round 13:** 1 ch, 1 dc in 1st dc, [5 ch, miss 3 dc, 1 dc in next dc] to end, omitting last dc, ss in 1st dc.

**Round 14:** Ss in each of 1st 3 ch, 7 ch, 1 dtr, 3 ch in each 5 ch sp to end, ss in 4th ch. Fasten off.

**Round 15:** This round is made up of separate flower motifs joined to Round 14 as they are worked.

## 1st motif

Wind yarn around finger to form a ring.

**1st motif round:** (RS) 4 ch, leaving last loop of each st on hook, work 4 dtr in ring, yrh and pull through 5 loops on hook, [5 ch, 5dtrcl in ring] 3 times, 2 ch, 1 tr in 1st sp after join of 14th round, 2 ch, 5dtrcl in ring, 2 ch, 1 tr in last sp of Round 14, 2 ch, 5dtrcl in ring, 5 ch, ss in 4th ch. Fasten off.

## 2nd motif

Work as 1st motif but making 1st and 2nd joins in 3rd and 2nd sps from previous join, then join in the same way to adjacent 5 ch sp of previous motif after working 6th petal. Make 17 more motifs joining to edge and previous motif in the same way as 2nd motif.

| | |
|---|---|
| • | ss |
| o | ch |
| + | dc |
| † | tr |
| ‡ | dtr |
| 🌐 | 5dtrcl |

*This charted stitch pattern shows the first*
*14 rounds of the waistcoat.*

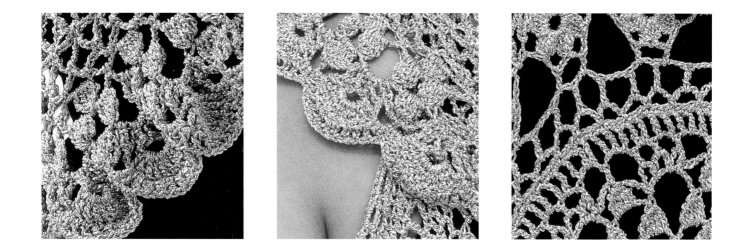

## 20th motif

Work as 1st motif until 3 petals have been completed, join in 1st motif between 3rd and 4th petals, then join to edge and previous motif in the same way as 2nd motif.

With RS facing, join yarn in 1st 5ch sp before join between 1st and 2nd motifs.

**Round 16:** 5 ch, 1 tr in same sp, 2 ch, 1 dtr in joined sp of 1st motif, 2 ch, * 1 trtr over join between motifs, 2 ch, 1 dtr in first joined sp of next motif, 2 ch, [1 tr, 2 ch] twice in each of next two 5 ch sps, 1 dtr in last joined sp of motif, 2 ch, rep from * 18 more times, 1trtr over join between motifs, 2 ch, 1 dtr in first joined sp of first motif, 2 ch, [1 tr, 2 ch] twice next 5 ch sp, ss in 3rd ch.

**Round 17:** 4 ch, 1 tr in first sp, 1 ch, [1 tr in next st, 1 ch, 1 tr in foll sp] to end, ss in 3rd ch.

**Round 18:** 6 ch, [1 dtr in next tr, 2 ch] 3 times, * leaving last loop of each st on hook, work 1 dtr in each of next 5 tr, yrh and pull through 6 loops on hook, 2 ch, [1 dtr in next tr, 2 ch] 9 times, rep from *, 19 more times, ending last rep [1 dtr in next tr, 2 ch] 5 times, ss in 4th ch.

**Round 19:** 4 ch, 1 dtr in 1st sp, [1 dtr in next dtr, 1 dtr in next sp] 3 times, * miss 5dtrcl, [1 dtr in next sp, 1 dtr in next dtr] 9 times, 1 dtr in foll sp, rep from * 19 times, ending last rep [1 dtr in next sp, 1 dtr in next dtr] 5 times, 1 dtr in foll sp, ss in 4th ch. [380 sts.]

**Round 20:** 1 ch, 1 dc in same place as ss, 7 ch, miss 2 dtr, 1 dc in next dtr, 7 ch, miss 2 dtr, * 1 dc in each of next 2 dtr, [7 ch, miss 2 dtr, 1 dc in next dtr] 5 times, 7 ch, miss 2 dtr, rep from * 18 times, 1 dc in each of next 2 dtr, [7 ch, miss 2 dtr, 1 dc in next dtr] 3 times, 3 ch, miss 2 dtr, 1 dtr in 1st dc.

### 2nd and 3rd sizes

**Next round:** 1 ch, 1 dc in dtr, [7 ch, 1 dc in next 7 ch sp] to end, 3 ch, 1 dtr in 1st dc.

### 3rd size

Work last round again.

### All sizes

120 7 ch sps.

**Armhole round:** 1 ch, 1 dc in dtr, [4 ch, 1 dc in next 7 ch sp] 17 (19:21) times, make 64 (69:74) ch, miss next 12 (13:14) 7 ch sps for left armhole, 1 dc in next 7 ch sp, [4 ch, 1 dc in next 7 ch sp] 77 (73:69) times, make 64 (69:74) ch, miss next 12 (13:14) 7 ch sps for right armhole, ss in 1st dc.

## FRONTS AND COLLAR

**Round 1:** 1 ch, 1 dc in 1st dc, [7 ch, 1 dc in next dc] to left armhole, * [7 ch, 1 dc in armhole sp] 12 (13:14) times *, [7 ch, 1 dc in next dc] to right armhole, rep from * to *, 3 ch, 1 dtr in 1st dc.

**Round 2:** 1 ch, 1 dc in dtr, [7 ch, 1 dc in next 7 ch sp] to end, 3 ch, 1 dtr in 1st dc.

**Round 3:** 1 ch, 1 dc in dtr, [4 ch, 1 dc in next 7 ch sp] to end, 4 ch, ss in 1st dc.

**Round 4:** 1 ch, 1 dc in 1st dc, [7 ch, 1 dc in next dc] to end, 3 ch, 1 dtr in 1st dc.

Work Rounds 2, 3 and 4 two more times, then work Rounds 2 and 3 one (two:three) more times.

## EDGING

**Round 1:** Ss in 1st 4 ch sp, 4 ch, leaving last loop of each st on hook, work 4 dtr in 1st 4 ch sp, yrh and pull through 5 loops on hook, [5 ch, 1 dc in next 4 ch sp, 5 ch, 5dtrcl in foll 4 ch sp] 59 times, 5 ch, 1 dc in last 4 ch sp, 5 ch, ss in 4th ch.

**Round 2:** Ss in 1st 5 ch sp, 4 ch, leaving last loop of each st on hook, work 4 dtr in 1st 5 ch sp, yrh and pull through 5 loops on hook, [7 ch, 5dtrcl in next 5 ch sp, 4 ch, 5dtrcl in foll 5 ch sp] 59 times, 7 ch, 5dtrcl in last 5 ch sp, 1 dtr in 4th ch.

**Round 3:** Ss in dtr sp, 4 ch, leaving last loop of each st on hook, work 4 dtr in dtr sp, yrh and pull through 5 loops on hook, * [5 ch, 1 dc in next 7 ch sp] 4 times, 5 ch, 5dtrcl in next 4 ch sp, rep from * 58 times, [5 ch, 1 dc in last 7 ch sp] 4 times, 5 ch, ss in 4th ch.

**Round 4:** 1 ch, 1 dc in same place as ss, * 3 ch, miss next 5 ch sp, 1 tr in next 5 ch sp, 3 ch, [1 tr, 3 ch] twice in next 5 ch sp, 1 tr in

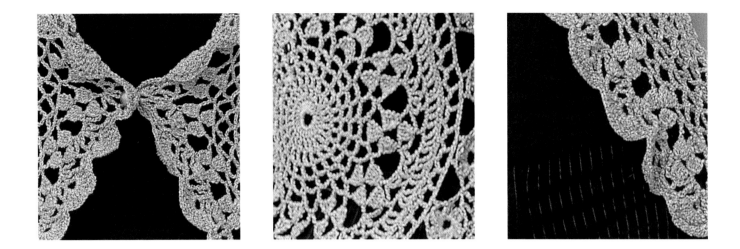

next 5 ch sp, 3 ch, miss next 5 ch sp, 1 tr in 5dtrcl, rep from * 59 times omitting 1 tr at end of last rep, ss in 1st dc.

**Round 5:** Ss in 1st 3 ch sp, 1 ch, [3 dc in 3 ch sp, miss next 3 ch sp, 9 dtr in foll 3 ch sp, miss next 3 ch sp, 3 dc in foll 3 ch sp, 1ch] 60 times, ss in 1st dc.

**Round 6:** * 1 ch, [1 tr, 1 ch] in each of next 9 dtr, 1 dc in 1 ch sp, rep from * 59 times, ending last rep ss in 1st ch.
Fasten off.

### ARMHOLE EDGINGS

With RS facing, join yarn at right under arm.
**Row 1:** [4 ch, 1 dc in next 7 ch sp of last round of back] 12 (13:14) times, 4 ch, ss in dc. Do not turn.

**Round 1:** Ss in 1st 4 ch sp of front, work 4 dc in each 4 ch sp around armhole, ss in 1st dc.
Fasten off.
With RS facing, join yarn at left shoulder and complete in same way as right armhole edging.

### TO MAKE UP

Darn in ends. Try on waistcoat and decide on best place to fasten front, sew button on a fan on right front and slip button through hole in corresponding fan on left front.

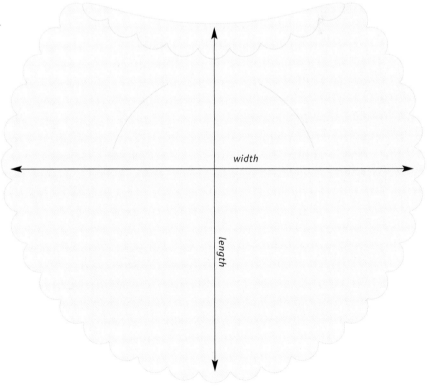

# FRILLED MOHAIR WRAP

*The openwork centre of this lightweight wrap is in Solomon's knot stitch which gives a lacy effect but is easy to work. Solomon's knot stitch is really just a series of elongated double crochet stitches. The frilled edging is in treble crochet.*

*The hook size is quite large for the thickness of the yarn. Work loosely to make it easier to insert hook when making the knots.*

*To help keep the length of the loop for each knot the same, extend the stitch, then hold it between finger and thumb while working the locking stitch. If you make your stitches a different length, you may need a different amount of yarn.*

*There is no foundation chain for Solomon's knot stitch.*

*If you want to make the scarf without the frill you'll need just one ball of yarn.*

## HELPFUL HINTS

- Working with mohair isn't difficult as long as you tension the yarn and make the stitches loosely.
- If you need to pull back, ease the stitches apart, don't pull or the hairs will cling together.
- The centre of the wrap will grow quickly because the stitches are so big and open.

## MEASUREMENTS

**Actual width (with frill)**
61 cm
24 in
**Actual length (with frill)**
164.5 cm
64¾ in

## MATERIALS

- 4 × 25 g balls of Rowan Kidsilk Haze in Candy Girl 606
- 4.00 mm crochet hook

## TENSION

A group of four Solomon's knots measure 4.5 cm (1¾ in), 16 sts to 10 cm (4 in), 3 rows to 3.5 cm (1½ in) over treble using 4.00 mm hook. Change hook size if necessary to obtain this tension.

## ABBREVIATIONS

*See page 9.*

## WRAP

Make a slip knot on the hook and work 1 ch.
**Row 1:** * Draw loop on hook up to 2 cm (¾ in), yrh and pull through, insert hook between loop and back strand, yrh and pull through to make 2 loops on hook, yrh and pull through, one knot has been completed, rep from * until 26 knots have been made.
**Row 2:** Miss the knot on the hook and the next 3 knots, 1 dc in centre of next knot, * make 2 knots, miss 1 knot in Row 1, 1 dc in next knot, rep from * to end of row making last dc in 1 ch at beg of Row 1. There are 12 four-knot groups along short edge of wrap.
**Row 3:** Make 3 knots, 1 dc in next unjoined knot of previous row, * make 2 knots, 1 dc in next unjoined knot of previous row, rep from * to end.
Row 3 forms Solomon's knot stitch patt. Cont in patt until there are 35 four-knot groups along long edge of wrap. Fasten off.

## EDGING

Join yarn at one corner of wrap.
**Round 1:** Ss in 1st 2-knot sp, 3 ch, 14 tr in same 2-knot sp, work 15 tr in each 2-knot sp around edge of wrap, ss in 3rd ch.
**Round 2:** 3 ch, 1 tr in 3rd ch, [2 tr in each tr] to end, ss in 3rd ch.
**Round 3:** 3 ch, [1 tr in each tr] to end, ss in 3rd ch. Fasten off. Darn in ends.

*The size of each panel of the lacy pattern reduces to make this flattering, waistcoat flare out at the lower edge. The ribbon yarn alternates between matt cotton and shiny nylon giving a subtle change of texture as the fabric catches the light.*

# LONG POINTED-EDGE WAISTCOAT

🖐 *Each point is worked separately. The points are joined and the waistcoat is worked in one to the armholes, then divided for back and fronts.*

🖐 *The flare on the waistcoat is made by reducing the amount of chain between treble group fans so the lower part of the waistcoat is more open. After working 5 rows in treble fan pattern without any chain between, the width is further reduced by changing down a hook size.*

## HELPFUL HINTS
- It's easier to see the stitches in dark yarn if you work with a piece of light coloured fabric on your lap.
- If you prefer, fasten the waistcoat with a flower corsage, a brooch or even a tie cord made from left-over yarn

## MEASUREMENTS
### To fit bust
| | | | |
|---|---|---|---|
| 76–86 | 91–102 | 107–117 | cm |
| 30–34 | 36–40 | 42–46 | in |

### Actual width
| | | | |
|---|---|---|---|
| 86 | 105.5 | 125 | cm |
| 34 | 41½ | 49 | in |

### Actual length
| | | | |
|---|---|---|---|
| 74.5 | 78 | 81 | cm |
| 29 | 30¾ | 32 | in |

*In the instructions figures are given for the smallest size first; larger sizes follow in brackets. Where only one set of figures is given this applies to all sizes.*

## MATERIALS
- 6 (8:10) × 50 g balls of Sirdar Duet in Black 745
- 6.00 mm and 5.50 mm crochet hooks
- 1 m (39 in) silk organza ribbon and 0.5 m (20 in) velvet ribbon (optional)

## TENSION
Each 7-row point measures 14 cm (5½ in) wide and 8 cm (3 in) high, 15 sts and 6 rows to 10 cm (4 in) measured over 1 ch tr fan patt using 6.00 mm hook, 18 sts and 6 rows to 10 cm (4 in) over tr fan patt using 5.50 mm hook. Change hook sizes if necessary to obtain these tensions.

## ABBREVIATIONS
*See page 9.*

# WAISTCOAT

## BACK AND FRONTS
**1st point** Wrap yarn around finger to form a ring. Use 6.00 mm hook.
**Row 1:** 3 ch, [1 tr, 1 ch, 2 tr] in ring, pull end to close ring and turn.
**Row 2:** (RS) Ss in each of first 2 tr, ss in 1 ch sp, 3 ch, 1 tr in 1 ch sp, [1 ch, 2 tr] twice in 1 ch sp.
**Row 3:** Ss in each of first 2 tr, ss in first 1 ch sp, 3 ch, [1 tr, 1 ch, 2 tr] in first 1 ch sp, 2 ch, [2 tr, 1 ch, 2 tr] in second 1 ch sp.
**Row 4:** Ss in each of first 2 tr, ss in first 1 ch sp, 3 ch, [1 tr, 1 ch, 2 tr] in first 1 ch sp, 2 ch, [2 tr, 1 ch, 2 tr] in 2 ch sp, 2 ch, [2 tr, 1 ch, 2 tr] in last 1 ch sp.
**Row 5:** Ss in each of first 2 tr, ss in first 1 ch sp, 3 ch, [1 tr, 1 ch, 2 tr] in first 1 ch sp, 3 ch,

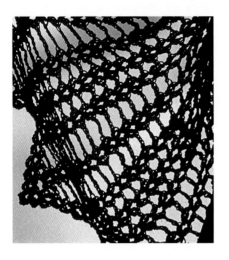

[2 tr, 1 ch, 2 tr] in centre 1 ch sp, 3 ch, [2 tr, 1 ch, 2 tr] in last 1 ch sp.

**Row 6:** Ss in each of first 2 tr, ss in first 1 ch sp, 3 ch, [1 tr, 1 ch, 2 tr] in first 1 ch sp, 4 ch, [2 tr, 1 ch, 2 tr] in centre 1 ch sp, 4 ch, [2 tr, 1 ch, 2 tr] in last 1 ch sp.

**Row 7:** Ss in each of first 2 tr, ss in first 1 ch sp, 3 ch, [1 tr, 1 ch, 2 tr] in first 1 ch sp, 5 ch, [2 tr, 1 ch, 2 tr] in centre 1 ch sp, 5 ch, [2 tr, 1 ch, 2 tr] in last 1 ch sp.

Fasten off.

### 2nd, 3rd, 4th, 5th, 6th, 7th and 8th points

Work as 1st point but before fastening off work 2 (3:4) ch, ss in 3rd ch at beg of Row 7 of previous point.

### Join edging points

With RS facing, join yarn in 1st 1 ch sp of right front point.

**Row 1:** (RS) 3 ch, [1 tr, 1 ch, 2 tr] in first 1 ch sp, 5 ch, [2 tr, 1 ch, 2 tr] in next 1 ch sp, 5 ch, * [2 tr, 1 ch, 2 tr] in foll 1 ch sp, [1 ch, 2 tr] 2 (4:6) times in 2 (3:4) ch sp between points, 1 ch [2 tr, 1 ch, 2 tr] in next 1 ch sp, 5 ch, [2 tr, 1 ch, 2 tr] in foll 1 ch sp, 5 ch, rep from * 6 more times, [2 tr, 1 ch, 2 tr] in last 1ch sp.

**Row 2:** Ss in each of first 2 tr, ss in first 1 ch sp, 3 ch, [1 tr, 1 ch, 2 tr] in first 1 ch sp, * 5 ch, [2 tr, 1 ch, 2 tr] in next 1 ch sp, 5 ch, [2 tr, 1 ch, 2 tr] in foll 1 ch sp, [1 ch, miss 1 ch, 2 tr, 1 ch, 2 tr in foll 1 ch sp] 2 (3:4) times, rep from * 6 more times, 5 ch, [2 tr, 1 ch, 2 tr] in next 1 ch sp, 5 ch, [2 tr, 1 ch, 2 tr] in last 1 ch sp. [31 (38:45) tr fans.]

Row 2 forms the 5 ch tr fan patt. Patt 4 more rows.

**Next row:** Ss in each of first 2 tr, ss in first 1 ch sp, 3 ch, [1 tr, 1 ch, 2 tr] in first 1 ch sp, * 4 ch, [2 tr, 1 ch, 2 tr] in next 1 ch sp, 4 ch, [2 tr, 1 ch, 2 tr] in foll 1 ch sp, [1 ch, miss 1 ch, 2 tr, 1 ch, 2 tr in foll 1 ch sp] 2 (3:4) times, rep from * 6 more times, 4 ch, [2 tr, 1 ch, 2 tr] in next 1 ch sp, 4 ch, [2 tr, 1 ch, 2 tr] in last 1 ch sp.

This row forms the 4 ch tr fan patt.

Patt 4 more rows.

**Next row:** Ss in each of first 2 tr, ss in first 1 ch sp, 3 ch, [1 tr, 1 ch, 2 tr] in first 1 ch sp, * 3 ch, [2 tr, 1 ch, 2 tr] in next 1 ch sp, 3 ch, [2 tr, 1 ch, 2 tr] in foll 1 ch sp, [1 ch, miss 1 ch, 2 tr, 1 ch, 2 tr in foll 1 ch sp] 2 (3:4) times, rep from * 6 more times, 3 ch, [2 tr, 1 ch, 2 tr] in next 1 ch sp, 3 ch, [2 tr, 1 ch, 2 tr] in last 1 ch sp.

This row forms 3 ch tr fan patt.

Patt 3 more rows.

**Next row:** Ss in each of first 2 tr, ss in first 1 ch sp, 3 ch, [1 tr, 1 ch, 2 tr] in first 1 ch sp, * 2 ch, [2 tr, 1 ch, 2 tr] in next 1 ch sp, 2 ch, [2 tr, 1 ch, 2 tr] in foll 1 ch sp, [1 ch, miss 1 ch, 2 tr, 1 ch, 2 tr in foll 1 ch sp] 2 (3:4) times, rep from * 6 more times, 2 ch, [2 tr, 1 ch, 2 tr] in next 1 ch sp, 2 ch, [2 tr, 1 ch, 2 tr] in last 1 ch sp.

This row forms 2 ch tr fan patt.

Patt 2 more rows.

**Next row:** Ss in each of first 2 tr, ss in first 1 ch sp, 3 ch, [1 tr, 1 ch, 2 tr] in first 1 ch sp, * 1 ch, [2 tr, 1 ch, 2 tr] in next 1 ch sp, 1 ch, [2 tr, 1 ch, 2 tr] in foll 1 ch sp, [1 ch, miss 1 ch, 2 tr, 1 ch, 2 tr in foll 1 ch sp] 2 (3:4) times, rep from * 6 more times, 1 ch, [2 tr, 1 ch, 2 tr] in next 1 ch sp, 1 ch, [2 tr, 1 ch, 2 tr] in last 1 ch sp.

This row forms 1 ch tr fan patt.

Patt 1 more row.

**Next row:** Ss in each of first 2 tr, ss in first 1 ch sp, 3 ch, [1 tr, 1 ch, 2 tr] in first 1 ch sp, * [2 tr, 1 ch, 2 tr] in next 1 ch sp, [2 tr, 1 ch, 2 tr] in foll 1 ch sp, [miss 1 ch, 2 tr, 1ch, 2 tr in foll 1 ch sp] 2 (3:4) times, rep from * 6 more times, [2 tr, 1 ch, 2 tr] in next 1 ch sp, [2 tr, 1 ch, 2 tr] in last 1 ch sp. [31 (38:45) tr fans, 155 (190:225) sts.]

The last row forms tr fan patt. Patt 5 rows. Change to 5.50 mm hook. Patt 2 rows.

## RIGHT FRONT

**Row 1:** (RS) Ss in each of first 2 tr, ss in 1st 1 ch sp, 3 ch, 1 tr in 1st 1 ch sp, [2 tr, 1 ch, 2 tr] in each of next 5 (7:9) 1 ch sps, 2 tr in foll 1 ch sp, turn and complete right front on these sts.

**Row 2:** 3 ch [2 tr, 1 ch, 2 tr] in each of next 5 (7:9) 1 ch sps, 1 tr in 3rd ch.

**Row 3:** Miss 1st tr, ss in each of next 2 tr, ss in

1st 1 ch sp, 3 ch, [1 tr, 1 ch, 2 tr] in 1st 1 ch sp, [2 tr, 1 ch, 2 tr] in each of next 4 (6:8) 1 ch sps.

**Row 4:** Ss in each of first 2 tr, ss in first 1 ch sp, 3 ch, [1 tr, 1 ch, 2 tr] in 1st 1 ch sp, [2 tr, 1 ch, 2 tr] in each of next 3 (5:7) 1 ch sps, 2 tr in last 1 ch sp.

**Row 5:** 3 ch, [2 tr, 1 ch, 2 tr] in each of next 4 (6:8) 1 ch sps.

**Row 6:** Ss in each of first 2 tr, ss in first 1 ch sp, 3 ch, [1 tr, 1 ch, 2 tr] in first 1 ch sp, [2 tr, 1 ch, 2 tr] in each of next 3 (5:7) 1 ch sps.

**Row 7:** Ss in each of first 2 tr, ss in 1 ch sp, 3 ch, 1 tr in first 1 ch sp, [2 tr, 1 ch, 2 tr] in each of next 3 (5:7) 1 ch sps.

**Row 8:** Ss in each of first 2 tr, ss in first 1 ch sp, 3 ch, [1 tr, 1 ch, 2 tr] in first 1 ch sp, [2 tr, 1 ch, 2 tr] in each of next 2 (4:6) 1 ch sps, 1 tr in 3rd ch.

**Row 9:** Miss 1st tr, ss in each of next 2 tr, ss in first 1 ch sp, 3 ch, [1 tr, 1 ch, 2 tr] in first 1 ch sp, [2 tr, 1 ch, 2 tr] in each 1 ch sp to end. [3 (5:7) fans, 15 (25:35) sts.]

### 2nd and 3rd sizes only

Cont in patt, dec at front edge in same way as Rows 4 and 5 on next 2 rows. Work next row in same way as Row 6.

### 3rd size only

Cont in patt, dec at front edge in same way as Rows 7 and 8 on next 2 rows. Work next row in same way as Row 9.

*It's easy to keep track of how many rows of each of the chain and treble fan patterns you've worked if you place markers at each end of the last row each time you change patterns.*

*Each treble fan is made up of 2 tr, 1 ch, 2 tr. Remember to count each fan as 5 sts when checking your tension.*

### All sizes

[3 (4:5) fans, 15(20:25) sts.] Patt 3 (2:1) rows.
Fasten off.

### BACK

With RS facing, miss 1 ch sp of fan at right
underarm and join yarn in next 1ch sp.

**Row 1:** (RS) 3 ch, 1 tr in same 1 ch sp as
joined yarn, [2 tr, 1 ch, 2 tr] in each of next
13 (16:19) 1 ch sps, 2 tr in next 1 ch sp, turn
and complete back on these sts.

**Row 2:** 3 ch, [2 tr, 1 ch, 2 tr] in each of next
13 (16:19) 1 ch sps, 1 tr in 3rd ch.

**Row 3:** Miss 1st tr, ss in each of next 2 tr, ss in
first 1 ch sp, 3 ch, [1 tr, 1 ch, 2 tr] in first 1 ch
sp, [2 tr, 1 ch, 2 tr] in each 1 ch sp to end.
[13 (16:19) fans, 65 (80:95) sts.]
Cont in tr fan patt, work 9 (11:13) more rows.
Fasten off.

### LEFT FRONT

With RS facing, miss 1 ch sp of fan at left
underarm and join yarn in next 1 ch sp.

**Row 1:** (RS) 3 ch, 1 tr in same 1 ch sp as
joined yarn, [2 tr, 1 ch, 2 tr] in each of next
5 (7:9) 1 ch sps, 2 tr in last 1 ch sp.

**Row 2:** 3 ch, [2 tr, 1 ch, 2 tr] in each of next
5 (7:9) 1 ch sps, 1 tr in 3rd ch.

**Row 3:** Miss 1st tr, ss in each of next 2 tr, ss in
1st 1 ch sp, 3 ch, [1 tr, 1 ch, 2 tr] in 1st 1 ch
sp, [2 tr, 1 ch, 2 tr] in each of next 4 (6:8)
1 ch sps.

**Row 4:** Ss in each of first 2 tr, ss in first 1 ch sp, 3 ch, 1 tr in 1st 1 ch sp, [2 tr, 1 ch, 2 tr] in each of next 4 (6:8) 1 ch sps.

**Row 5:** Ss in each of first 2 tr, ss in first 1 ch sp, 3 ch, [1 tr, 1 ch, 2 tr] in first 1 ch sp, [2 tr, 1 ch, 2 tr] in each of next 3 (5:7) 1 ch sps, 1 tr in 3rd ch.

**Row 6:** Miss 1st tr, ss in each of next 2 tr, ss in first 1 ch sp, 3 ch, [1 tr, 1 ch, 2 tr] in first 1 ch sp, [2 tr, 1 ch, 2 tr] in each of next 3 (5:7) 1 ch sps.

**Row 7:** Ss in each of first 2 tr, ss in 1st 1 ch sp, 3 ch, [1 tr, 1 ch, 2 tr] in first 1ch sp, [2 tr, 1 ch, 2 tr] in each of next 2 (4:6) 1 ch sps, 2 tr in last 1 ch sp.

**Row 8:** 3 ch, [2 tr, 1 ch, 2 tr] in each of next 3 (5:7) 1 ch sps.

**Row 9:** Ss in each of first 2 tr, ss in first 1 ch sp, 3 ch, [1 tr, 1 ch, 2 tr] in first 1 ch sp, [2 tr, 1 ch, 2 tr] in each 1 ch sp to end.
[3 (5:7) fans, 15 (25:35) sts.]

### 2nd and 3rd sizes only

Cont in patt, dec at front edge in same way as Rows 4 and 5 on next 2 rows. Work next row in same way as Row 6.

### 3rd size only

Cont in patt, dec at front edge in same way as Rows 7 and 8 on next 2 rows. Work next row in same way as Row 9.

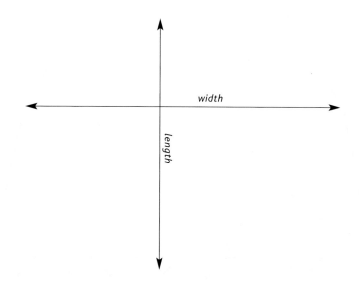

### All sizes

[3 (4:5) fans, 15 (20:25) sts.] Patt 3 (2:1) rows. Fasten off.

### TO MAKE UP

Matching sts, join shoulders. Leaving two long ends of the organza ribbon, make up a double bow from the two ribbons, slip ends through the last pattern before the start of the front shaping and tie.

*Keep your shoulders cosy in this flattering, shapely shrug. It's in simple treble with a little shell edging and given a touch of luxury by the soft cotton and angora mix yarn.*

# SHELL-EDGED SHRUG

✋ *The shrug is worked in two sections and joined at the centre back. It is designed to fit very closely.*

✋ *Working a dc and 2 ch in the first treble instead of the usual 3 ch at the start of a row helps to close the gap after the first stitch.*

✋ *Joining the sleeve and working a chain extension to use for both back and front stitches is neater than sewing the side seam.*

✋ *When shaping the back and front, omitting the chain usually worked at the beginning of a row automatically decreases a stitch as there is no end chain to work into on the next row.*

## HELPFUL HINTS
- If you prefer, you could fasten your shrug with a brooch instead of a button.
- Always take the yarn end from the centre of the ball.

## MEASUREMENTS
### To fit bust

| | | |
|---|---|---|
| 81–86 | 91–97 | cm |
| 32–34 | 36–38 | in |

### Actual width

| | | |
|---|---|---|
| 80 | 90.5 | cm |
| 31½ | 35½ | in |

### Actual length (including edging)

| | | |
|---|---|---|
| 33 | 35.5 | cm |
| 13 | 14 | in |

### Actual sleeve
51 cm
20 in

*In the instructions figures are given for the smaller size first; larger size follows in brackets. Where only one set of figures is given this applies to both sizes.*

## MATERIALS
- 7 (8) × 50 g balls of Debbie Bliss Cotton Angora in red 14
- 4.50 mm crochet hook
- 1 button

## TENSION
13 sts to 10 cm (4 in) and 15 rows to 20 cm (8 in) measured over treble crochet using 4.50 mm hook. Change hook size if necessary to obtain this tension.

## ABBREVIATIONS
**2trtog** – leaving last loop of each st on hook, work 1 treble in each of next 2 sts, yrh and pull through 3 loops on hook
**3trtog** – leaving last loop of each st on hook, work a treble in each of next 3 sts, yrh and pull through 4 loops on hook
*See also page 9.*

# SHRUG

## LEFT SIDE

### Make starting chain for cuff edging
Make 54 (58) ch.
**Row 1:** (WS) Working into top strand only, work 1 dc in 2nd ch from hook, 1 dc in each ch to end. [53 (57) sts.]
**Row 2:** 1 ch, ss in 1st dc, [miss 1 dc, 4 tr in next dc, miss 1 dc, ss in next dc] to end, do not turn, ss in side of Row 1.

### Sleeve
**Row 1:** (RS) Ss in 1st starting ch, 3 ch, [1 tr in each of next 3 ch, miss 1 ch] 12 (13) times, 1 tr in each of last 4 ch. [41 (44) sts.]

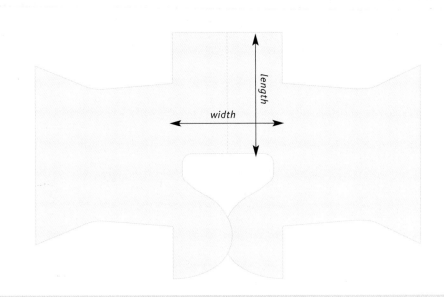

width

length

There is no need to make a buttonhole, simply slip the button between the treble stitches at right front point.

**Row 2:** 1 dc in 1st tr, 2 ch, 1 tr in each tr to last st, 1 tr in 3rd ch.

This row forms tr patt.

Working into 2nd ch at end of foll rows, cont in tr, work 6 more rows.

**Dec row:** (RS) 1 dc in 1st tr, 2 ch, 2trtog, 1 tr in each tr to last 3 sts, 2trtog, 1 tr in 2nd ch. [39 (42) sts.]

Cont in tr, dec in this way at each end of next 4 RS rows. [31 (34) sts.]

Cont in tr, work 4 rows.

**Inc row:** (WS) 3 ch, 1 tr in 1st tr, 1 tr in each tr to last st, 2 tr in 2nd ch. [33 (36) sts.]

Cont in tr, inc in this way at each end of 6 foll WS rows, then at each end of next 3 rows. [51 (54) sts.]

### Shape for back and front

Ss in top of 3 ch to join top of sleeve. [17 (19) ch.]

**Next row:** (WS) Working into top loop only of ch, 1 tr in 4th ch from hook, 1 tr in each of next 13 (15) ch, 1 tr in each of 51 (54) sts of sleeve, 1 tr in each of next 15 (17) ch. [81 (88) sts.] Cont in tr, work 8 (10) rows **.

### Back

**Row 1:** (RS) 1 dc in 1st tr, 2 ch, 1 tr in each of next 39 (43) tr, turn and complete back on these 40 (44) sts.

**Dec row 1:** (WS) 1 dc in 1st tr, 1 tr in each tr to last st, 1 tr in 2nd ch.

**Dec row 2:** 1 dc in 1st tr, 2 ch, 1 tr in each tr to last 2 tr, 2trtog.

[38 (42) sts.] Cont in tr, work 3 more rows.

Fasten off.

### Front

With RS facing, miss next 19 (20) tr and join yarn in next tr.

**Row 1:** (RS) 3 ch, 1 tr in each tr to end. [22 (24) sts.]

**Dec row 1:** 1 dc in 1st tr, 1 tr in each tr to last 2 sts, 2trtog. [20 (22) sts.]

Cont in tr, dec one st in this way at each end of next 2 (3) rows. [16 sts.]

**Dec row 2:** 1 dc in 1st tr, 2trtog, 1 tr in each tr to last 3 sts, 3trtog. [12 sts.]

Cont in tr, dec 2 sts in this way at each end of next 2 rows. [4 sts.]

Dec one st at each end of next row. [2 sts.]

Fasten off.

### RIGHT SIDE

Work as given for left side to **.

### Front

**Row 1:** (RS) 1 dc in 1st tr, 2 ch, 1 tr in each of next 21 (23) tr, turn and work on these 22 (24) sts. Complete as given for left front from Dec row 1.

### Back

With RS facing, miss next 19 (20) tr and join yarn in next tr.

**Row 1:** (RS) 3 ch, 1 tr in each tr to end. [40 (44) sts.]

**Dec row 1:** (WS) 1 dc in 1st tr, 2 ch, 1 tr in each tr to last 2 sts, 2trtog.

**Dec row 2:** 1 dc in 1st tr, 1 tr in each tr to last st, 1 tr in 2nd ch. [38 (42) sts.] Cont in tr, work 3 more rows. With RS together, join back seam with dc.

### EDGING

With RS facing, join yarn at right side seam.

**Round 1:** (RS) 1 ch, spacing sts evenly, work 36 (44) dc in row-ends to right front point, 18 (21) dc to neck edge, 19 (20) dc up right front neck, 26 dc across back neck, 19 (20) dc down left front neck, 18 (21) dc to left front point, 36 (44) dc to left side seam and 60 (68) dc across back, ss in 1st dc, turn. [232 (264) sts.]

**Round 2:** 1 ch, 1 dc in each dc to end, ss in 1st dc, turn.

**Round 3:** 1 ch, ss in 1st dc, [miss 1 dc, 4 tr in next dc, miss 1 dc, ss in next dc] to end, working last ss in 1st st. Fasten off.

### TO MAKE UP

Join sleeve seams. Sew on button.

*A pretty sweetheart neckline and a cut-away back make this easy-to-work vest very special. The vest fabric is in a simple stitch pattern with rows of double crochet and filet mesh alternating to give an open but stable fabric. Add sequins for a fabulous night time look.*

# SEQUINNED VEST TOP

★ ☆ ☆ VERY EASY

*Always join in a new ball of yarn at the side edge, not in the middle of a row.*

*Do not count the 1 ch at the start of dc rows as a stitch.*

*Increases are made on filet rows but stitch counts are given after the following dc row as this is easier than remembering to count spaces on the filet row as a stitch.*

*When working straight, the filet rows start with a dc and 3 ch so the first hole in the mesh is the same size as the others.*

## HELPFUL HINTS

- The vest is worked from the top down. This makes shaping the front neck easier and avoids the possibility of a tight lower edge.
- The pattern is very simple but because the rows are not the same it's easy to know which is a right side row when shaping.
- Cathay is a cotton, viscose and silk mix yarn with a lovely sheen and is available in twelve jewel-like shades. The sequins are sewn on afterwards, so you can match the sequins to the yarn, add any mix of sequin shapes and colours you like or you could decorate the vest with beads instead.
- If you don't want to add the sequins, you can layer the vest over a t shirt for a more sporty, daytime look.

## MEASUREMENTS
### To fit bust

| | | | |
|---|---|---|---|
| 81–86 | 91–97 | 102–107 | cm |
| 32–34 | 36–38 | 40–42 | in |

### Actual width

| | | | |
|---|---|---|---|
| 87.5 | 101 | 110 | cm |
| 34½ | 39¾ | 43 | in |

### Actual length

| | | | |
|---|---|---|---|
| 51.5 | 53 | 54.5 | cm |
| 20¼ | 21 | 21½ | in |

*In the instructions figures are given for the smallest size first; larger sizes follow in brackets. Where only one set of figures is given this applies to all sizes.*

## MATERIALS
- 5 (6:7) × 50 g balls of Debbie Bliss Cathay in purple 12
- 4.00 mm crochet hook
- approximately 600 large paillette sequins (optional)

## TENSION
18 sts and 13 rows to 10 cm (4 in) measured over filet and dc patt using 4.00 mm hook. Change hook size if necessary to obtain this tension.

## ABBREVIATIONS
*See page 9.*

# VEST

## BACK
Make 36 (40:44) ch.

**Row 1:** (WS) 1 dc in 2nd ch from hook, 1 dc in each ch to end. [35 (39:43) sts.]

**Row 2:** (RS) 1 dc in 1st dc, 3 ch, miss 1 dc, 1 tr in next dc [1 ch, miss 1 dc, 1 tr in next dc] to end.

**Row 3:** 1 ch, 1 dc in 1st tr, [1 dc in next 1 ch sp, 1 dc in next tr] to last 2 sts, 1 dc in last

1 ch sp, 1 dc in 2nd ch.
Rows 2 and 3 form the filet and dc patt.
Patt 12 more rows, ending with a dc row.

### Shape armholes

**Inc row:** (RS) 4 ch, 1 tr in 1st dc, [1 ch, miss 1 dc, 1 tr in next dc] to end, 1 ch, 1 tr in last dc again.

**Next row:** 1 ch, 1 dc in 1st tr, [1 dc in next 1 ch sp, 1 dc in next tr] to last tr, 1 dc in 4 ch sp, 1 dc in 3rd ch. [39 (43:47) sts.]
Cont in patt, inc in this way on next 6 (7:8) RS rows. [63 (71:79) sts.]
Do not turn at end of last row, make 9 (11:11) ch, turn.

**Next row:** (WS) 1 dc in 2nd ch from hook, 1 dc in each of next 7 (9:9) ch, 1 dc in 1st tr, [1 dc in next 1 ch sp, 1 dc in next tr] to last tr, 1 dc in 4 ch sp, 1 dc in 3rd ch, remove hook and using spare yarn make 8 (10:10) ch, slip loop of last dc back on to hook and work 1 dc in each of next 8 (10:10) ch. [79 (89:99) sts.]
** Cont in patt, work straight for 18 rows.

**Dec row 1:** (RS) 1 dc in 1st tr, 2 ch, miss 1st dc, [1 tr in next dc, 1 ch, miss 1 dc] to last 3 dc, 1 tr in next dc, miss 1 dc, 1 tr in last dc.

**Dec row 2:** 1 ch, miss 1st dc, [1 dc in next tr, 1 dc in next 1 ch sp] to last tr, 1 dc in last tr. [75 (87:95) sts.]
Patt 4 rows straight. Work 1st and 2nd dec rows again. [71 (83:91) sts.]
Patt 12 rows straight. Fasten off.

### FRONT

### First side

**Strap:** Make 4 ch.
**Row 1:** (WS) 1 dc in 2nd ch from hook, 1 dc in each of next 2 ch. [3 sts.]
**Row 2:** 1 dc in 1st dc, 3 ch, miss 2nd dc, 1 tr in 3rd dc.
**Row 3:** 1 ch, 1 dc in tr, 1 dc in sp, 1 dc in 2nd ch.
Rows 2 and 3 form strap patt.
Patt 12 more rows.

### Shape front

**Row 1:** 4 ch, 1 tr in 1st dc, 1 ch, miss 2nd dc, 1 tr in 3rd dc, 1 ch, 1 tr in 3rd dc again.
**Row 2:** 1 ch, 1 dc in 1st tr, [1 dc in next 1 ch sp, 1 dc in next tr] twice, 1 dc in last 4 ch sp, 1 dc in 3rd ch. [7 sts.]
**Row 3:** 4 ch, 1 tr in 1st dc, [1 ch, miss 1 dc, 1 tr in next dc] 3 times, 1 ch, 1 tr in last dc again.
**Row 4:** 1 ch, 1 dc in 1st tr, [1 dc in next 1 ch sp, 1 dc in next tr] 4 times, 1 dc in last 4 ch sp, 1 dc in 3rd ch. [11 sts.]
**Row 5:** 4 ch, 1 tr in 1st dc, [1 ch, miss 1 dc, 1 tr in next dc] to end, 1 ch, 1 tr in last dc again.
**Row 6:** 1 ch, 1 dc in 1st tr, 1 dc in 1st sp, [1 dc in next tr, 1 dc in next sp] to end, 1 dc in 3rd ch. [15 sts.]
Cont in filet and dc patt, increasing as set at each end of next 4 (5:6) RS rows.
[ 31 (35:39) sts.] Fasten off.

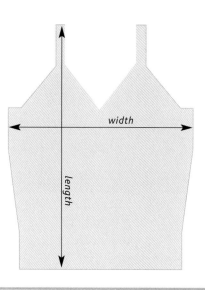

*width*

*length*

## Preparation for armhole

Without turning work, join yarn at opposite end of last row and make 8 (10:10) ch. Fasten off.

## Second side

Work as given for first side but do not fasten off after last row.

## Preparation for armhole

Do not turn, make 9 (11:11) ch, turn.
**Joining row:** (WS) Across second side work 1 dc in 2nd ch from hook, 1 dc in each of next 7 (9:9) ch, * 1 dc in 1st tr, 1 dc in 1st 1 ch sp, [1 dc in next tr, 1 dc in next sp] 14 (16:18) times, 1 dc in 3rd ch *, 1 ch, rep from * to * across first side, 1 dc in each of 8 (10:10) ch. [79 (91:99) sts.]
Complete as given for back from ** to end.

## NECK EDGING

Matching sts, join shoulders. With RS facing, join yarn at right shoulder seam.
**Round 1:** 1 ch, 1 dc in each of 29 (33:37) dc across back neck, 41 (44:47) dc in row-ends to centre front, 1 dc in 1 ch sp at centre front, 41 (44:47) dc in row-ends to right shoulder, ss in 1st dc, do not turn.
**Round 2:** Work crab st (dc backwards) in each st to end. Fasten off and darn in ends.

## ARMHOLE EDGINGS

Join side seams. With RS facing, join yarn at side seam.
**Row 1:** (RS) 1 ch, 1 dc in each ch along armhole edge, 41 (44:47) dc in row-ends to shoulder, 41 (44:47) dc in row-ends to armhole edge, 1 dc in each ch to side seam, ss in 1st dc, do not turn.
**Round 2:** Work crab st (dc backwards) in each st to end, fasten off and darn in ends.

## LOWER EDGING

With RS facing, join yarn at side seam and work in crab st (dc backwards) around lower edge. Fasten off and darn in ends.

## TO DECORATE

Using a slim, sharp needle, sew sequins on front of vest, following the filet rows but scattering the sequins so some of the crochet fabric shows. If you secure each sequin with several small over-sew stitches there's no need to fasten off each time you sew on a sequin, simply slip the needle along the back of the crochet stitches to place the next sequin.

*To space the dc evenly around neck and armhole edgings, work 1 dc in each dc row-end and 2 dc in each filet row-end.*

*There's no need to buy matching thread to sew on the sequins, simply cut a length of Cathay and tease out the separate strands.*

*The sequins used in the picture have holes at the top so they hang down when sewn on.*

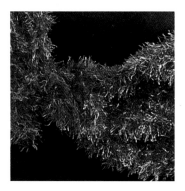

# FUNKY FUR CAPELET

*Keep bare shoulders warm with this neat little wrap or wear it on top of a sweater for instant glamour.*

*There is no right or wrong side to the fabric.*

*Working a dc and 2 ch into the first treble stitch instead of the usual 3 turning chain helps to close the gap between the first and second stitches. Loosen the loop on the hook slightly before working the dc. Work the 2nd chain a little bit loosely as this will make it easier to work into on the next row.*

*Placing markers on the last increase row makes it easier to measure the length of the wrap.*

## HELPFUL HINTS

- You can join in new yarn anywhere during a row, just work over the ends and they will be hidden in the dense pile.
- The wrap is in treble crochet. The furry texture hides the stitches so when you need to count rows, hold the work up to the light.
- Use the end from the centre of the ball; the furry strands will pull through more smoothly as you crochet.

## MEASUREMENTS
### Actual width
20 cm

8 in
### Actual length (excluding ties)
96 cm

38 in

## MATERIALS
- 4 × 50 g balls of Sirdar Funky Fur in Inky Blue 530
- 4.00 mm crochet hook

## TENSION
18 sts and 11 rows to 10 cm (4 in) measured over treble using 4.00 mm hook. Change hook size if necessary to obtain this tension.

## ABBREVIATIONS
**2trtog** – leaving last loop of each st on hook, work 1 tr in each of next 2 sts, yrh and pull through all 3 loops on hook

**4trtog** – work in same way as 2trtog in each of 4 sts, yrh and pull through all 5 loops on hook
*See also page 9.*

# WRAP

### First tie
**Row 1:** Make one ch quite loosely, then make 3 more ch, work 3 tr in 1st ch. [4 sts.]

**Row 2:** 1 dc in 1st tr, 2 ch, 1 tr in 1st tr, 1 tr in each of next 2 tr, 2 tr in 3rd ch. [6 sts.]

**Row 3:** 1 dc in 1st tr, 2 ch, 1 tr in each tr to last st, 1 tr in 2nd ch.

Row 3 forms treble crochet. Cont in tr, work 10 more rows.

### Shape front
**Inc row 1:** 1 dc in 1st tr, 2 ch, 1 tr in 1st tr, 2 tr in each of next 4 tr, 2 tr in 2nd ch. [12 sts.]

**Inc row 2:** 1 dc in 1st tr, 2 ch, 1 tr in 1st tr, 2 tr in each of next 10 tr, 2 tr in 2nd ch. [24 sts.]

Cont in tr, inc one st in same way as Row 2 of tie at each end of next 6 rows. [36 sts.]

Place markers at each end of last row.

Cont in tr, work straight until wrap measures 82 cm (32¼ in) from markers.

### Shape front

**Dec row 1:** 1 dc in 1st tr, 2 ch, 2trtog, 1 tr in each tr to last 3 sts, 2trtog, 1 tr in 2nd ch. [34 sts.]

Cont in tr, dec in this way at each end of next 5 rows. [24 sts.]

**Dec row 2:** [2trtog] 12 times. [12 sts.]

**Dec row 3:** [2trtog] 6 times. [6 sts.]

### Second tie

Cont in tr, work 11 rows. Dec one st in same way as before at each end of next row. [4 sts.] 4trtog. Work 1 ch. Fasten off.

Simple filet mesh takes on a glamorous look in metallic yarn decorated with beads. Whatever you're wearing, add this jewelled scarf for instant party!

# BEADED EVENING SCARF

## HELPFUL HINTS
- Working with beads isn't difficult as long as you choose beads that slide easily along the yarn.
- Tip the beads out on to a shallow dish, then it's easy to pick them up without spilling them.
- You can use a mix of different beads or you could match the colour of the beads to your outfit.
- Joining in new thread while making the fringe could leave a weak place, so take about 4 m (157 in) of gold thread and join the centre of the thread to the centre stitch of the short edge of the scarf to make two lengths and work out from the centre.

## MEASUREMENTS
Actual width (without beads)
6 cm
2½ in
Actual length (including tassels)
150 cm
59 in

## MATERIALS
- 2 × 25 g balls of Coats Anchor Arista in gold 300
- 2.50 mm crochet hook
- 340 medium size matt and shiny glass beads
- 440 small glass beads and 22 larger beads
- gold sewing thread
- long, slim needle

## TENSION
10 beaded filet spaces of 1 dtr, 1B, plus 1 dtr at end measure 9 cm (3½ in), 10 filet spaces of 1 dtr, 1 ch, plus 1 dtr at end measure 6 cm (2½ in), 8 rows to 10 cm (4 in) over filet patt using 2.50 mm hook. Change hook size if necessary to obtain this tension.

## ABBREVIATIONS
**1B** – slide a bead up close to the work and elongating loop on hook, work 1 ch to hold bead in place
*See also page 9.*

## SCARF

Make slipknot on hook, [1ch, 1B] 10 times, 5 ch, turn.
**Row 1:** [1B, 1 dtr in ch between beads] 9 times, 1B, 1 dtr in last ch.
**Row 2:** 4 ch, [1B, 1 dtr in next dtr] 9 times, 1B, 1 dtr in 4th ch.
Row 2 forms beaded filet patt.
Working last dtr in 4th ch, work 14 more rows. 170 beads have been used. Cont with unbeaded yarn, joining in 2nd ball and sliding beads along until needed.

*Thread 170 of the larger beads on to the first ball of yarn and the remaining 170 on to the second ball before starting to work the scarf. To do this, thread a slim needle with a short length of sewing cotton, tie the ends in a knot to make a loop and slide the knot to one side. Pass the end of the yarn through the loop, pick up the beads with the needle a few at a time and slide them down on to the yarn.*

*The fringe uses smaller gold glass beads, plus a rocaille bead at the end of each strand.*

**Next row:** 5 ch, [1 dtr in next dtr, 1 ch]
9 times, 1 dtr in 4th ch.
This row forms filet patt. Work 79 more rows
with unbeaded yarn, then work 17 rows of
beaded filet patt. Fasten off.

## FRINGE

Using a long, slim needle and leaving half of
the thread free, join a four metre length of
gold sewing thread to the centre stitch of one
short end of the scarf. Pick up 20 beads with
the needle and slide them up close to the
work, pick up one larger bead, then taking
thread over this bead, slip needle down
through the smaller beads, pull thread to
tension beads so the strand is flexible but
there are no gaps and secure with a few small
oversew stitches. Slip needle through edge of
scarf to next stitch in the filet pattern and
repeat until each filet stitch is finished with a
strand of small beads. Fringe the other end in
the same way.

# SUPPLIERS AND USEFUL ADDRESSES

**UK**

Coats Crafts UK
PO Box 22
Lingfield House
Lingfield Point
McMullen Road
Darlington
DL1 1YQ
Tel: (01325) 394394
Email: enquiries.ccuk@coats.com
www.coatscrafts.co.uk
*Suppliers of Coats and Patons
yarns. Call for your nearest stockist*

Creative Beadcraft
Unit 2
Asheridge Business Centre
Asheridge Road
Chesham
Buckinghamshire
HP5 2PT
Tel: (01494) 778818
www.creativebeadcraft.co.uk
*Mail order supplier of beads,
sequins and other trimmings*

Designer Yarns Ltd
Units 8-10
Newbridge Industrial Estate
Pitt Street
Keighley
West Yorkshire
BD21 4PQ
Tel: (01535) 664222
Fax: (01535) 664333
Email: jane@designeryarns.uk.com
www.designeryarns.uk.com
*Suppliers of Debbie Bliss and Noro
yarns. Call for your nearest stockist*

Ells and Farrier
20 Beak Street
London
WF1 9RE
Tel: (020) 7629 9964
*Bead supplier*

Quadra UK Ltd
Tey Grove
Elm Lane
Feering
Essex
CO5 9ES
Tel: (01376) 573802
Email: quadrauk.com
*Suppliers of Elle yarns.
Call for your nearest stockist*

Rowan Yarns
Green Lane Mill
Holmfirth
West Yorkshire
HD9 2DX
Tel: (01484) 681881
Fax: (01484) 687920
Email: mail@knitrowan.com
www.knitrowan.com
*Call for details of your nearest
stockist or order online*

Sirdar Spinning
Flanshaw Lane
Alverthorpe
Wakefield
West Yorkshire
WF2 9ND
Tel: (01924) 371501
Fax: (01924) 290506
Email: orders@sirdar.co.uk
www.sirdar.co.uk
*Call for details of your nearest
stockist or order online*

## USA

Knitting Fever Inc.
PO Box 502
Roosevelt
New York 11575
Tel: (516) 546 3600
Fax: (516) 546 6871
Email: webmaster@knittingfever.com
*Stockist of Sirdar yarns*

Rowan USA
4 Townsend West
Suite 8
Nashua
New Hampshire 03064
Tel: (603) 886 5041/5043
Email wfibers@aol.com
*Call for details of your nearest
stockist*

## AUSTRALIA

Australian Country Spinners
314 Albert Street
Brunswick
Victoria 3056
Tel: (03) 9380 3888
*Stockist of Rowan yarns*

Creative Images
PO Box 106
Hastings
Victoria 3915
Australia
Tel: (03) 5979 1555
Fax: (03) 5979 1544
Email:
creative@peninsula.starway.net.au
*Stockist of Sirdar yarns*

## SOUTH AFRICA

Arthur Bales Ltd
62 4th Avenue
Linden
Johannesburg 2195
Tel: (027) 118 882 401
Fax: (027) 117 826 137
Email: Arthur@new.co.za
*Stockist of Rowan yarns*

Saprotex International (Pty)
PO Box 1293
East London 5200
Tel: (027) 43 763 1551
Fax: (027) 43 763 1929
Email: tbarratt@bertrand.co.za
*Stockist of Sirdar yarns*

# INDEX

## ACKNOWLEDGEMENTS

A huge thank you to everyone who helped me with this book. First of all, David Rawson for mentioning my name, Rosemary Wilkinson for giving me the opportunity to work on this project and Clare Sayer for her patience and enthusiasm. Thanks to Sian Irvine for the lovely photographs, as well as to the models: Emma, Jo, Kat, Natalie and Sarah. Isobel Gillan did a wonderful job designing the book as well.

Special thanks to David Rawson and all at Sirdar Spinning; Debbie Bliss and all at Designer Yarns; Kate Buller

and all at Rowan, Coats and Patons and Mike Cole at Elle for the inspirational yarns.

Thank you to Sally Buss, Pauline Webster and Hilary Swaby for help with creating the garments and to Betty Speller, for her encouragement and for the lovely patchwork gilet. Thank you to Sue Horan, the pattern checker, who did a thorough job, as ever.

And finally, I would like to dedicate this book to my mother, Hilda Griffiths, who taught me to knit and to crochet.

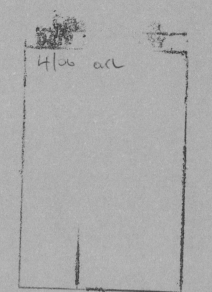

4/06 arl